D1468385

What Works

A Guide to
Environmental Education and
Communication Projects
for Practitioners and Donors

Edited by Martha C. Monroe

NEW SOCIETY PUBLISHERS

With grateful appreciation to William Stapp who helped bring a vision of environmental education to so many people around the world.

Cataloguing in Publication Data:
A catalog record for this publication is available from the National Library of Canada.

Cover design by Richard Chartier.

Printed in Canada on acid-free, partially recycled (20 percent post-consumer) paper using soy-based inks by Transcontinental/Best Book Manufacturers.

New Society Publishers acknowledges the financial support of the Government of Canada through the Book Publishing Industry Development Program (BPIDP) for our publishing activities, and the assistance of the Province of British Columbia through the British Columbia Arts Council.

Paperback ISBN: 0-86571-405-3

Inquiries regarding requests to reprint all or part of *What Works* should be addressed to New Society Publishers at the address below.

To order directly from the publishers, please add $4.00 shipping to the price of the first copy, and $1.00 for each additional copy (plus GST in Canada). Send check or money order to:
  New Society Publishers
  P.O. Box 189, Gabriola Island, B.C. V0R 1X0, Canada

New Society Publishers aims to publish books for fundamental social change through nonviolent action. We focus especially on sustainable living, progressive leadership, and educational and parenting resources. Our full list of books can be browsed on the worldwide web at: http://www.newsociety.com

NEW SOCIETY PUBLISHERS
Gabriola Island, B.C., Canada

Education for Sustainability

What Works is one of New Society Publisher's
Education for Sustainability series of books copublished with
the Academy for Educational Development (AED).
Books in this series focus specifically on strategies for educating
professionals, local officials, activists, and the general public about ways to
promote effective sustainability at all levels:
local, regional, national and international.

AED is an independent, nonprofit organization with 38 years
experience in fostering domestic and global solutions to urgent social, health,
agricultural, and environmental problems.
A recognized leader in social marketing and behavior change theory, AED has
worked in more than 120 countries worldwide, cooperating with USAID, the
World Bank, and other international agencies.

Academy for Educational Development
1825 Connecticut Avenue, NW
Washington, DC 20009-5721, USA
www.aed.org

New Society Publishers
PO Box 189, Gabriola Island
BC, V0R 1X0, Canada
www.newsociety.com

Table of Contents

7   Acknowledgments
8   Preface
9   Introduction

19 CHAPTER 1 — FOSTERING SUSTAINABLE DEVELOPMENT IN COMMUNITIES

20 From Research to Conservation in the Eastern Amazon
    Margaret Cymerys — United States

22 CADIPSA: Conservation and Development in Sparsely Populated
    Areas of Europe
    Ramon Lastra — Switzerland

24 Inspiring Pride and Protection in a Brazilian Protected Area
    Marcus Polette — Brazil

26 Managing Watersheds in Benin
    Constant Dangbegnon — Benin

28 Sustainable Development in Rural Ecuador through Conservation
    Education
    Clarice Strang — Ecuador

30 Environmental Education for Tanzania: A Practical Success Story
    Mary Shuma — Tanzania

32 Ecocultural Tourism in Lombok, Indonesia
    Rocky Rohwedder — United States

35 CHAPTER 2 — CREATING CHANGE IN SCHOOL SYSTEMS

36 Training Key Education Personnel in Environmental Education in India
    Abdul Ghafoor Ghaznawi — Pakistan

38 A Participatory Process for the Integration of Environmental Education
    into the Primary School Curriculum in Brazil
    Lou Ann Dietz and Vera Rodrigues — United States and Brazil

40 Environmental Education in the Senegalese School System
    Mamadou Diaw — Senegal

42 "Ecologizing" Education in Russia
    Margarita Arutiunian — Russia

44 Environmental Curriculum Development in Elementary Schools
    in Bulgaria
    Veleslava Tzakova — Bulgaria

46 "Old Sable:" A Russian-American Environmental Education Project
    Linda Rhines and Michael Brody — United States

49   CHAPTER 3 — USING MASS MEDIA

50   Formative Research Shapes an Environmental Campaign in Egypt
Orlando Hernádez — United States

52   The Environmental Journalist Seminar: A Communications Tool for Conservation
Patricia B. Kelly — United States

54   Promoting Conservation Awareness through Electronic Media
Katarina Panji — Indonesia

56   Educational Documentaries as the Centerpiece of Informational Campaigns
Haroldo Castro — United States

58   "Sëkó:" Mass Media for a National Environmental Ethic in Costa Rica
Guillermo A. Canessa-Mora, Luis Fernando Rojas, and Osvaldo Valerin — Costa Rica

61   CHAPTER 4 — FOSTERING ENVIRONMENTAL POLICY

62   Combatting Desertification in Pakistan with Environmental Communication Strategies
Syed Jamil Hasan Kazmi — Pakistan

64   Advocacy for the Reform of Forest Management Policy in the Philippines
Chris Seubert — United States

66   Conserving Sonoran Coastal Wetlands through Public Involvement and Environmental Education
Mariana Lazcano-Ferrat — Mexico

68   Stopping Illegal Trafficking of Wildlife in Guatemala
Myriam Monterroso — Guatemala

71   CHAPTER 5 — SUPPLEMENTING FORMAL EDUCATION

72   Adapting Environmental Education Materials for Hungary
Andrea Deri and Jamie Watts — Hungary and United States

74   Environmental Education for Primary School Teachers in Mexico
Lizbeth Baqueiro — Mexico

76   Preserving Traditions and Acting for the Future: Environmental Education and Sakha Youth
Valentina Dmitrieva — Russia

78   "Action" for Growing Minds in Southern Africa
Stephen R. Murray — Zimbabwe

80   The Air Quality of Curitiba: Evaluating and Educating
Ziole Zanotto Malhadas — Brazil

82   Changing Attitudes through EDUCAR, A Radio Environmental Education Program
Suyapa Dominguez Merlo and Jaime Bustillo — Honduras

84   Implementing Education Programs to Conserve Biodiversity:
Lessons from Mongolia
Jessica Bernstein — United States

87   **CHAPTER 6 — ORGANIZING NONFORMAL ENVIRONMENTAL EDUCATION**

88   OUTREACH: Disseminating and Evaluating Information
Packets Worldwide
James V. Connor — United States

90   Changes in Water Conservation Beliefs and Practices through
After-School Programs in Jordan
Nancy Diamond and Orlando Hernández — United States

92   Puppet Shows as a Tool in Environmental Education Programs
Flavio Linares — Guatemala

94   Folk Media: A Nonformal Environmental Education Strategy in
the Philippines
Roscela Pamela S. Poyatos — Philippines

96   Using Environmental Education Activities to Reach Aboriginal School
Children in Taroko National Park, Taiwan
Homer C. Wu — Taiwan

98   Connecting Wetland Ecosystems, Cultures, and Migratory Birds
through Sister Schools
Heather Johnson and Cathy Rezabeck — United States

101   **CHAPTER 7 — BUILDING LOCAL CAPACITY**

102   Female Adult Literacy in Rural Pakistan
Sabiha S. Daudi — United States

104   Dissemination of Environmental Materials and Training
Volodymyr Tykhyi — Ukraine

106   EE-TIPs: Making the Most of U.S. Environmental Education Resource
Distribution in Eastern and Central Europe
Joan Haley — United States

108   The Challenge of Changing Teaching Styles in Rural Zimbabwe
Kathy Greaves Stiles — Zimbabwe

110   Second Generation Leadership: A Nicaragua-Wisconsin Partners
Environmental Leadership Project
Joe Passineau and Dan Sivek — United States

112   Environmental Management in the Kyrgyz Republic
John H. Baldwin — United States

114   **SUMMARY**

115   Region and Country Index

116   Contact List

Acknowledgments

The guidelines suggested in this book stem from years of work in the field and from the examples of successful projects described on the following pages. Each project represents a presentation at GreenCOM's International EE&C Workshop at the annual conference of the North American Association for Environmental Education, (NAAEE) in November 1996 in Burlingame, California. The descriptions are purposefully brief; they are intended to spark ideas, paint pictures of possibilities, and provide concrete examples of successful projects. The presenter or contact person listed on pages 116-120 can be contacted for additional information.

While every effort was made to capture these cases accurately, no doubt some nuances and details were lost in translation. We offer our apology to the project coordinators and funders for any inaccuracies.

Martha C. Monroe
University of Florida

Carole Douglis
GreenCom

Brian Day
GreenCom

The workshop was organized by
GreenCOM's staff:
Brian A. Day, Project Director
Martha C. Monroe, Resource Center Director
Dana Inerfeld, Program Associate

This book was compiled with assistance from
an additional team of people:
Leslie Comnes, Copy-Editor
Amanda Robins, Program Associate
Renny Seidel, Advising Editor
Richard Chartier, Graphic Designer
Paulina Espinosa, Program Associate
Miyoun Lim, Intern
Carole Douglis, Editorial Consultant

Workshop Registration and Logistics:
North American Association for
  Environmental Education

Workshop Co-Sponsors:
United States Agency for International
Development, through
GreenCOM, The Environmental Education and
  Communication Project
Conservation International
Global Vision
National Consortium for Environmental
  Education and Training, University of Michigan
North American Institute for Environmental
  Information and Communication (CICEANA)
United States Peace Corps
Worldwide Fund for Nature (WWF)
World Conservation Union (IUCN)
World Resources Institute
World Wildlife Fund—United States

Preface

The Academy for Educational Development (AED) has been using Environmental Education and Communications (EE&C) for nearly a decade to improve our domestic and international environment. To introduce a broad audience to what EE&C can do, AED has produced this collection of wonderful examples of what works from across the globe.

These outstanding case studies are drawn from an international workshop sponsored by the United States Agency for International Development through GreenCOM — its Environmental Education and Communication Project. AED is proud to be the prime contractor for GreenCOM.

GreenCOM builds on more than two decades of experience AED has in applying social marketing and behavior change theory to domestic and global education, social, health, agriculture and environmental problems.

AED is excited to present to practitioners and donors alike these examples of real projects that have made a real difference in people's lives and their environment. We hope that you will find this book helpful in your work.

Stephen F. Moseley
President and Chief Executive Officer
Academy for Educational Development

Introduction

Puppet shows in Guatemala bring smiles to the faces of young and old even as the characters speak of the disastrous consequences of deforestation. Call-in radio shows explain conservation initiatives in Indonesia and build public support for biodiversity in selected conservation areas. Teachers along Mexico's Sonoran coastal wetlands help their students learn about this valuable ecosystem and launch habitat restoration activities. Eco-club members in Jordanian secondary schools explore home water conservation and measure their families' water consumption.

Around the world, educational efforts and communication strategies are informing people of environmental issues, supporting positive efforts, and involving people in decisions about sustainable environmental practices. These projects vary enormously, from documentary television specials to handmade posters, and from small community projects to national education reform campaigns.

The fact that environmental education and communication (EE&C) programs vary so widely can make the process of developing and funding new projects a challenge. While it would be convenient to have a simple formula for effective environmental education, both humans and their environments are much too diverse to be accurately generalized. Despite the differences in medium, scale, and context of EE&C projects, however, there are strong similarities among successful environmental education and environmental communication activities. This book highlights these common threads, examples of strategies that work, and guidelines for developing new projects.

The cases published here were presented at an international workshop at the annual conference of the North American Association for Environmental Education on November 1 and 2 of 1996. This workshop, Using Environmental Communications to Make Sustainable Development Happen, attracted 150 participants from over 30 countries. As nearly 50 different presenters described their education and communication projects, participants engaged in lively discussions about similar successes, strengths, and potential pitfalls. In the final discussion period, participants generated specific suggestions for the donor community that would increase the likelihood of successful project outcomes.

The next section of this book (pages 10-17) summarizes those suggestions. It is intended to provide program developers, managers, and funders with some concrete ideas about what works, what should be avoided, and how funding might be provided to environmental education and environmental communication efforts. The remainder of this book highlights the presentations from the workshop. These cases offer a glimpse at a wide variety of successful environmental efforts around the world.

For additional information about the projects, please communicate directly with the workshop presenters or the contact people listed on pages 116-120.

An Overview of Environmental Education and Environmental Communication Projects

To some people, environmental education and environmental communication are two terms for the same type of programs. Others, however, draw clear boundaries between the two. In the field, they form a continuum of practices with the ends being distinctly different, and the middle forming a murky muddle of similar skills and strategies. Some agencies solve this problem by grouping these similar activities together as EE&C (environmental education and communication). No matter what their label, these activities and programs are designed to educate, empower, and involve an audience in resolving or preventing environmental issues.

Environmental education was formally defined at a UNESCO conference in Tbilisi, USSR, in 1977. It broadly refers to the activities that help develop a world population that is aware of and concerned about the total environment and its associated problems, and which has the knowledge, attitudes, motivations, commitments, and skills to work individually and collectively toward solving current problems and preventing new ones. Such programs may target decision makers, voters, architects, scouts, or teachers, and typically involve direct contact between the learners and the facilitators in educational experiences. Some environmental educators stress that they provide a balanced presentation of information and skills; they do not advocate for an environmentalist's position.

Both environmental education and communication recognize the complexity of human interactions with their environments, which include the economic, political, cultural and social systems in which people operate, as well as the natural systems. Environmental communication activities, however, are more likely to use information about these systems to shape unique campaigns to influence a target audience. While it has been defined more narrowly to mean the channels through which communication takes place, environmental communication has evolved to include a wide range of activities, strategies, and approaches. In practice, it can be similar to nonformal education and is increasingly becoming more interpersonal and participatory. Because information dissemination has had very weak links to behavior change, environmental communicators are developing new models that adapt advertising, public relations, social marketing, and consensus building techniques to be more effective at solving problems.

Key Elements of Successful EE&C Projects

Successful projects in either environmental education or environmental communication follow similar developmental strategies. These projects typically include increasing participation in the project design and implementation, pilot testing the materials and messages before launching the program, and monitoring the results of the project. The ways in which these programs are designed and implemented are very similar although different specific strategies may be used.

By examining successful projects, practitioners have become more certain of several ingredients that tend to insure success. Whether the projects involve mass media or individual instruction, successful projects generally include the following seven critical elements.

1. **Effective projects empower local communities and use their expertise.** Projects succeed only with the will and support of the people. There is a variety of ways to involve local communities in a project, including assessing their situation and viewpoints, encouraging their suggestions, enabling them to make good decisions, and helping them to share in the program benefits. Productive and meaningful participation takes time. While a project may streamline this process by using community representatives, care must be taken to ensure that these individuals truly represent the community. Real participation shares and converts decision-making power from the source to the disenfranchised; a successful project may be able to trace how the control of decisions changes over time as the community becomes more involved.

2. **Successful projects include scientific, social, economic, political, and cultural aspects.** Environmental issues are nested in an interdisciplinary mix of all these considerations. Because of their complexity, successful environmental education and communication activities are designed to include a variety of perspectives. For example, a project intended to conserve a wildlife species must also address the survival of local human communities, and a project supporting power generation must include safeguards for protecting the environment. While sometimes difficult to achieve, it is important to involve people who represent a variety of ethnicities and social classes, and both genders, as well as a variety of professional expertise.

3. **In successful projects, a variety of stakeholders are identified and integrally involved.** Successful projects bring a coalition of the stakeholders together to solve a problem, and these projects are designed to meet the stakeholders' needs. While it would be impractical for a large number of people to be consulted on every decision, successful projects invite stakeholders to participate in at least the beginning stages. Depending on the project, landowners, extension workers, teachers, curriculum developers, youth, elected officials, householders, farmers, and others can contribute appropriate

insights. Understanding the issue from a variety of perspectives may result in changing the focus or audience of the project.

4. **Successful projects aim to instill or support an environmental ethic as well as to assist residents in developing decision-making skills.** Projects are defined by the needs and resources of the local area, but whenever possible, successful projects move toward supporting an environmental ethic and developing decision-making skills. These aspects help communities participate in such activities as sustainable resource management, and help institutionalize a community's ability to identify and resolve environmental issues long after a project is completed. Although difficult and costly to evaluate, this is an appropriate goal for EE&C projects.

5. **Projects that are successful include a gender component.** For some years, policymakers have recognized that gender and environment are inextricably linked and that projects should formalize this connection. To some extent this has been accomplished through targeted programs focusing on the different social roles of men and women; for example, some programs focus on the fact that increasing deforestation causes women to walk further and spend a greater portion of their day getting the family's fuel and water. It is also important to recognize that women and men may have different, but important, perceptions, skills, and talents that need to be tapped for optimum decision-making on environmental issues.

6. **Successful projects are designed to be flexible and have a realistic timetable.** Good projects take time, and sufficient time must be built into the project design. As a project is implemented, the dynamics of the situation are bound to change; as skill building and education impact the community, the community's insights on the project will also change. A successful project needs to be designed to accommodate unforeseen changes. If a project is to involve stakeholders, it must be designed with options for change, so that people's involvement can truly make a difference.

7. **Effective projects are evaluated with appropriate tools.** Evaluation is critical to every project. Successful projects have a reasonable and meaningful match between the situation, the project goals, and the evaluation design. Sometimes the best outcome will come from the voices of the community members as they describe how their lives have changed through involvement with the project. Meaningful evaluation may at times be the number of people who receive a brochure; at other times it may be the commitment of the community to make change happen. Successful projects have measurable objectives that are relevant to the project's goals as well as feedback mechanisms to measure key variables throughout the project. These objectives may not be identified in the proposal, but should evolve from the early stages of data collection and stakeholder participation.

Recommendations for Specific Types of Projects

Because projects in environmental education and environmental communication can vary greatly, it is often helpful to think of the projects in terms of their general type, such as policy, nonformal education, or media projects. As a group, each type can offer insights into what works particularly well. The recommendations that follow come from years of work in the field and from the examples of successful projects described later in this book.

Fostering Sustainable Development in Communities

When villagers plant and tend community gardens, when local leadership launches an economic development plan, or when people seek ways to maintain wildlife populations for some monetary gain, environmental education and communication programs may be paving the way to increased knowledge and skills. Some knowledge will involve an increased awareness of the problem and potential solutions. Some skills will be procedural processes about how the change might be implemented. But additional skills in group leadership, communication, negotiation, and decision making are also important aspects of these development projects. As audiences for environmental education and communication programs gain environmental knowledge and skills, they can begin to implement appropriate changes in their lives and communities. Such changes should lead to a more sustainable lifestyle, though it is often difficult to foresee the outcome of these efforts when they are initiated. Like other activities described below, it is imperative that local people are involved in the design and leadership of EE&C programs to effect lasting change.

Projects that are designed to assist a community in reaching a more sustainable existence should:
- thoroughly assess the forces that create the existing conditions and that could influence the development process
- tap indigenous knowledge, particularly of women
- involve local residents and local leaders in the design and approval of the project
- provide training for local residents in the skills needed to critique the project, suggest helpful modifications, and embrace the approved version
- listen to what residents say they need and want, as well as to what experts say
- develop an education program to increase awareness about the problem and build skills to resolve the problem
- consider evaluating the project with indicators of community change, unless the project time-line is long enough to measure the ultimate changes intended.

Creating Change in School Systems

Projects that implement a broad, national environmental education curriculum seek to institutionalize environmental education by providing teacher training and certification, materials, supplemental resources, and national tests. School administrators, teachers, curriculum developers, and teacher educators are important audiences for these programs. Although school attendance is not universal, it is common in many nations, particularly at the primary school level; institutionalizing environmental education in this way can be an effective mechanism for building awareness, sharing knowledge, establishing skills, and helping communities take action. In many cases, the information and skills included in the change effort go beyond basic environmental information and cover local issues and conservation behaviors.

Projects involving systemic change in formal education policies should:
- develop or adapt curriculum locally, using outside resources to support local initiatives
- carefully analyze what is appropriate, starting with what people know and believe, and moving from there
- teach problem-solving skills by involving youth in the design and management of action projects
- identify and involve key stakeholders—those who can help a project succeed and can help sustain it over time
- support the institutionalization of environmental education by working toward national policies, teacher accreditation, sustainable teacher associations, improved teacher education institutions, local curriculum development, and quality education for girls
- increase the use of interactive, engaging teaching methods
- build in periodic review and evaluation procedures to help keep people involved in improving their educational program.

Using Mass Media

Mass media can be very effective partners for environmental management projects. Through broadcast media (television and radio), print media (newspapers, flyers, posters, billboards), and other media (hats, pencils, puppet shows, events), the public can be influenced with conservation messages. Well-designed messages, in conjunction with other supportive mechanisms, can win support for a new project or encourage new behaviors to protect a resource. It is critical that such projects include a preparatory analysis phase to understand the problem, the level of awareness, the audience's perspective, and how the media may best be used. Projects may also provide professional training and capacity building for the journalists themselves. Through such training, environmental issues may be more frequently and thoroughly reported. Interpersonal media (family members, neighbors, and opinion leaders speaking to individuals) can be a powerful tool to change individual behaviors, and can be triggered through a mass media campaign.

Such media projects could:
- invest in formative research to define the problem, the perspectives, and the audience for the communication campaign
- carefully pretest the messages with the intended audience to confirm their acceptance
- train media personnel in environmental issues and environmental reporting
- offer awards for the best environmental coverage
- include capacity building for local media personnel
- partner with other institutions to continue media work after the project is over
- build in a feedback mechanism so the public can discover how their efforts to change individual behaviors are affecting the resource.

Fostering Environmental Policy

Environmental policies will often be improved by engaging the citizenry in policy formation, using environmental communication activities to consult, advise, and include the public in the project planning process. Regulatory mechanisms can also be more effective when citizens are involved in deciding which changes to make in their environmental practices. Effective and sustainable environmental education and environmental communication programs can be integrated into national policy in other ways; some countries effectively add environmental components to national education standards, teacher training and certification requirements, curriculum development, and/or national testing.

In the early stages of using environmental education and environmental communication to support or change national policies:
- all stakeholders, particularly women, should be identified, invited, and included in the policy discussions
- discussions with stakeholders must be designed so that all voices have equal power, with an awareness of cultural norms that may silence or minimize some
- formative research should be conducted to understand the current situation, level of understanding of the issues, and climate for change
- efforts should concentrate on building local support among agencies, citizens, and organizations, particularly if the impetus for the policy is an international agreement or outside the nation's boundaries
- outside organizers must win the support, trust, and credibility of stakeholders.

Supplementing Formal Education

Many organizations and agencies work at the local level to provide teachers and youth with environmental education opportunities. This support is critical for several reasons: it provides in-service training for teachers, it creates a bank of local resources that help connect environmental concepts to each community, and it may be the only resource available, especially in nations without a national environmental education curriculum. As with nonformal education programs, a variety of models is readily available from around the world, but adapting these activities to the local culture with appropriate changes is a major task. In cases where the environmental issue is unique or the culture very influential, existing models may be irrelevant and materials development activities should begin anew.

Programs to develop supplemental resources should:
- meet the audience's needs for resources, accreditation, and training
- ascertain the acceptability of model curriculum and teaching activities, adapting where appropriate
- involve teachers and students in the design and dissemination
- allocate at least three years to develop and pretest materials, and longer if an evaluation of the final documents is planned
- creatively use local resources, local geography, and local connections
- teach about issues through a systematic and holistic approach to the environment, stressing connections rather than separate parts
- keep in mind that although the student is the ultimate recipient, the teacher is usually the program's audience; objectives and evaluation should focus on the teacher
- consider that materials for students be written with an entertaining storyline.

Organizing Nonformal Environmental Education

The audience and the strategies for nonformal education and communication programs are tremendously broad; they may include visitors to a park, resource managers receiving technical information from a government agency, or youth club members working on a service project. Many successful programs can provide tips for new projects, but few programs can be transplanted easily from one part of the world to another. Each culture and nation will bring its own unique contributions to the development of nonformal programs. Because such programs should be designed to meet local needs and to build local support, initial successes may come in very small steps. In fact, the entire project design may change as more local input is generated. Measurable success may only come over a longer time period.

Nonformal programs should:
- be designed to meet local needs after a needs assessment or formative research
- involve target audiences throughout program design
- use other nation's models for tips and clues
- provide information and skills, and opportunities to practice the skills through activities or service projects

- have a 5-10 year timeline rather than a 2-3 year one
- include environmental messages in the context of the organization's purpose and typical audience.

Building Local Capacity

Many development assistance projects include efforts to increase local capacity of agencies, organizations, and individuals to carry on their work as professional environmental educators and environmental communicators. Where capacity already exists, it can often benefit from professional development activities and exchanges. Professionals need the ability to share successes, explain projects, provide tips and suggestions, and learn from each other. The workshop from which these cases were assembled was one step in this direction, but participants called for more opportunities to increase their ability to conduct successful projects.

Future projects could:
- provide funding for the dissemination of project reports
- include funding for project leaders to travel to international meetings to share their work
- develop partnerships between education and communication professionals within a country or within a region
- enhance networks with existing environmental education and environmental communication associations
- establish communication mechanisms that do not rely on advanced technologies
- support regional exchange of experience between developing countries.

Conclusion

Few projects could successfully implement all of the recommendations and guidelines outlined above, and they are not intended as an exhaustive checklist. Most of these recommendations, however, do speak to the same few goals:
- involve appropriate people in the project design
- use the most appropriate strategies and the most current thinking for creating high-quality educational activities
- consider the larger picture of implications (both environmental and social)
- carefully evaluate the project to ascertain its effectiveness.

It is our hope that these guidelines and the cases that follow will help program managers design better proposals and will enable donors to fund more projects with confidence. We need not wait for a perfect formula for EE&C program design. We need only turn to successful projects to gain insight into what works, then share our knowledge broadly.

1 FOSTERING SUSTAINABLE DEVELOPMENT IN COMMUNITIES

Environmental education and communication programs that help communities understand their environment and make decisions that will lead to a sustainable future are critical contributions to international development programs. The following cases demonstrate a variety of techniques on nearly every continent with farmers, hunters, villagers, and fishers.

From Research to Conservation in the Eastern Amazon

Margaret Cymerys
Woods Hole Resarch Center/Instituto de Pesquisa
Ambiental da Amazonia
Point San Quentin, California

Along the Capim River in Brazil, community members living in the Amazon forest-margin attended workshops designed to help them choose wisely among several land-use options: logging, farming, ranching, and non-timber forest resource extraction.

The Situation

The Amazonian communities of the Capim River were colonized in the late 1800s. The people of these communities are agroextractivists who grow some crops and also extract fish, game, and fruits from the forest. They practice slash-and-burn agriculture growing farinha and manioc for flour, and, rarely, rice, beans, and corn. They hunt for paca, deer, and other wild game from the forest and rivers. Changes in the watershed have caused village hunters to notice a decline in native animal species. Cattle ranches cleared the surrounding forest in the region, putting pressure on the traditionally used forest and community lands. Since parks and

What Works

Involving local people in the collection of data about their resources helps strengthen their link to the issue.

Workshop activities, particularly interactive games, role playing, and discussions, confirm with local people the meaning of data and bring to light misconceptions or exaggerations.

The value of harvested resources is discussed in economic terms and compared to the cost of replacing these wild resources with purchased food.

Case studies and examples of how other communities protect resources help build ideas about possibilities.

Communities are empowered because they make decisions and implement this selection after careful consideration of information.

protected areas will be able to preserve only a small portion of the native biological diversity, local communities will always play an important role in the future of their forests and wildlife.

The Project

Preliminary discussions with hunters indicated that a healthy diversity of species remained in the community forests, so careful game management was still a possible strategy for protecting their hunting lifestyle. To help develop management plans, it was important to obtain the cooperation and involvement of local people.

The Forest and Communities Program of the Woods Hole Research Center and the local workers union, Sindicato dos Trabalhadores de Paragominas, developed a series of workshops to help communities make informed decisions about land-use options. Interactive workshops were designed with games, role playing, and discussions to convey game-population research results to the community, to promote forest conservation (particularly the benefits of using wildlife for food), and to facilitate community planning. The interactions helped the workshop facilitators assess the participants' understanding of the materials. For example, participants guessed the most commonly captured animals and created a pie chart of the species that are hunted. The audience's perceptions were fairly accurate, though a few more-prized species (deer and paca) were over-estimated.

Maps and posters helped explain where the animals were taken, indicating a clear habitat preference for forests, and even for certain tree species. The economic and nutritional value of the wildlife was calculated based on the need to replace this food source. The workshop also provided examples of actions other communities are taking with respect to game and forest management.

The Results

Success of the workshops is difficult to measure in the short term, but interviews with community members after the workshop indicated that 40% of the families relocated their agricultural clearings from primary forest to secondary forest. One community denied loggers access to their forest, voted not to divide the forest into individual plots, and is discussing the creation of a forest reserve.

CADISPA: Conservation and Development in Sparsely Populated Areas of Europe

Ramon Lastra
World Wide Fund for Nature (WWF) International
Gland, Switzerland

What Works

Environmental and economic concerns are addressed in ways that respect both conservation and development.

Education and training for adult decision makers and residents are vital to improving the quality of decisions about development and the environment.

Education programs for youth help make the community more aware of its valuable cultural and natural resources.

Rural communities across Europe suffer from environmental and cultural degradation. In this project, WWF supports rural efforts toward environmental and economic sustainability through environmental education and economic development.

The Situation

In 1988, WWF-United Kingdom wanted to start an educational project that would enable entire rural communities to make environmental decisions with insight and understanding. WWF worked with the Jordanhill campus of the University of Strathclyde for environmental education expertise, and the project was started on the windswept Scottish highlands and islands. The project, Conservation and Development in Sparsely Populated Areas (CADISPA), soon spread to Italy, Spain, Greece, and Portugal, helping local rural residents address specific conservation and development problems in their areas.

Despite thousands of years of human habitation, the sites in which CADISPA works have remained rural and undeveloped for good reasons: poor soils, inaccessibility, or the absence of mineral or water resources. These rural communities exist in the most marginal environments where small changes can have great impacts.

The Project

CADISPA is coordinated by WWF International and is partly funded by the European Union. The challenge for CADISPA is to help rural people come up with ways to use local resources to grow economically, while protecting the environment and preserving their cultural identity.

Each CADISPA project may be defined by a different language, culture, or economy, yet all the projects have the following characteristics:
- sparse populations subject to emigration and an aging population
- a damaged or precarious environmental balance threatened by development schemes such as dams, roads, bridges, intensive farming, forestry, or mass tourism
- poor, yet proud, residents who have a low capacity for self-defense
- active local environmental organizations ready to collaborate.

The Results

Several communities have achieved remarkable success through the project. Teachers and students participate in the program with natural resource conservation and environmental education activities. Local residents and policy makers are trained and motivated to lead the way to sustainable development. Increasing markets have revived crafts such as weaving, basketry, and embroidery.

Inspiring Pride and Protection in a Brazilian Protected Area

Marcus Polette
Universidade do Vale do Itaja
Santa Catarina, Brazil

The establishment of a protected area in southern Brazil in 1992 created conflicts in the neighboring community. After one year of research to understand the conflicts, including meetings with seven different sectors of the community, communication and education programs were designed to increase understanding and to promote a conservation ethic among children, teachers, fishers, tourists, and divers.

The Situation

Arvoredo Island and nearby islands are located in an archipelago in southern Brazil, in the state of Santa Catarina. The region was designated a protected area due to significant archaeological sites, high biodiversity, and a Naval Service lighthouse. The protection of the Arvoredo Coast Biological Reserve, however, generated conflict with the local fishers, tourists, and divers. To fully explore the variety of perspectives on the problem and to develop an educational strategy, Universidade do Vale do Itaja faculty conducted a significant research effort

What Works

A baseline for knowledge, awareness, and behavior enables one to understand the society, design an appropriate program, and later know if it was effective.

Working with teachers is an effective way to reach students: It is particularly helpful if the project can provide teaching materials.

Universities can be key to the development of EE programs. They can assist with the coordination of activities, the preparation of surveys and research tools, and the development of programs that maximize their resources with extension programs, researchers, faculty, and students.

Because environmental education is integrative and participatory, it provides a platform for all sectors to work toward safe, innovative solutions.

Posters, videos, and news releases can be inexpensive and yet very effective in underdeveloped regions.

including interviews of 869 people representing seven sectors of society. Difficulties encountered by the researchers included a lack of funding, no management plan, no infrastructure, and the isolation of the islands themselves, which makes them hard to reach.

The Program

The research helped create an environmental education program with three goals: to promote the environmental awareness in the school population (particularly first and second grade), to produce instructional material tailored to the local situation, and to train teachers in environmental education methodologies. The program for schools involves 44 district schools, reaching 10,000 children and teachers, and includes a video, books, and other instructional materials. Materials designed for the public include news bulletins, posters, brochures, signs, advertisements, and a photography exhibit seen by 300,000 people at shopping centers, parks, city halls, and festivals. These materials have helped communicate the importance of the environment. A workshop that helped teachers understand the problem and use the program was videotaped to be shared with other teachers.

The Results

After two and half years, Phase 1 of the project has brought education programs to 51 schools from 6 municipalities. A management committee has been established to organize segments of the society to protect the Reserve. Although posters and other print materials are effective and frequently used, teachers report that the video is their favorite resource.

For the last 200 years, fishers and divers have used the area that is now protected. Two years into this project, fishers agreed not to fish in the Biological Marine Reserve and divers are leading environmental education programs developed by the university for tourists.

The behavior change process will undoubtedly be time-consuming and will require a great deal of investment. Such a program can really work if the community is included in a participatory, transparent, and continuous process.

Managing Watersheds in Benin

Constant Dangbegnon
Université Nationale du Benin
Cotonou, Benin

What Works

The knowledge of stakeholders (in this case, indigenous people) can provide promising alternative perspectives to a complex problem such as water resource management.

A successful project pays particular attention to the cultural context of stakeholders.

Local farmers are more likely to seek information, learn new skills, and change their behavior when critical watershed resource management problems make sense to them and to their daily lives.

The quality of leadership among stakeholders contributes significantly to education and communication tasks; a successful project promotes and encourages the emergence of a stakeholder leader.

Decentralization of decision-making fosters more participation and focuses the research and development efforts on local people's needs and aspirations.

The "platform perspective" emphasizes stakeholders' knowledge in identifying appropriate actions for sustainable watershed management. In Benin, this approach was used with indigenous people to slow the rapid degradation and depletion of watershed resources.

The Situation

In northern and southern Benin, migrant farmers practice shifting cultivation as they clear and plant land, and then move to another piece of ground. Traditional knowledge governs the spacing of cultivated areas, the direction of the furrows, and the next piece of land that will be cleared. By tilling furrows in the direction of the sloping ground, farmers use the energy of the flowing water to clean the furrows of weed seeds. Unfortunately, this practice also contributes to erosion. In an effort to reduce soil erosion in one watershed, contour farming was introduced in the Mahi farming community. Contour farming contradicts indigenous practices because trees and shrubs are planted to maintain big ridges along contours. Since conventional extension activities fail to recognize the traditional knowledge and the context in which farmers make decisions, a more participatory approach was attempted in this project.

The Project

This research project was designed to use indigenous knowledge about farming and watershed management and to make recommendations for policy makers about communicating and facilitating environmental management projects. The approach respected local knowledge, particularly for coping with the risks involved in change. This perspective also helped stakeholders move from a defensive behavior to a communicative role, which facilitates responsible negotiation and decision-making.

After analyzing the different groups of farmers, it was clear that some farmers were not motivated to abandon their practice of shifting cultivation. One reason for this was that the migrant farmers are not land owners and were hesitant to make the investment required for contour farming. It was clear, however, that those who farmed degraded land could benefit from contour farming. After learning the benefits of this type of farming, several volunteers were willing to practice contour farming. Since the farmers perceived other issues (rural roads, clean water, health centers and schools) to be more important than soil erosion, the project provided limited investments for these improvements, and additional investments when the problem was more closely related to the watershed.

The volunteers followed the recommended procedure of planting cashew trees and vetiver shrubs on alternating contour lines, and annual crops like maize on secondary ridges. After one growing season, it was clear that maintaining the vetiver was too labor-intensive; the farmers much preferred to plant crops on contour lines that made an economic contribution to the farm (such as cashews and cajanus shrubs).

The Results

After three years of experience with farmers on watershed issues, the project organized a meeting of farmers from different villages. The participants realized that their small actions would not create a major impact on the watershed and that it would be better to coordinate efforts and join with other villages. A process has just begun to create the Inter-Villages Union for Management of Natural Resources (UIGREN).

Sustainable Development in Rural Ecuador through Conservation Education

Clarice Strang
Fundación Pro-Pueblo
Guayaquil, Ecuador

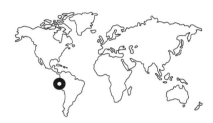

A broad community effort in western Ecuador is helping to restore traditional, sustainable farming techniques and to improve the standard of living of local communities. Education is partnered with concrete actions in community development to promote sustainable economic development.

The Situation

Western Ecuador is one of the world's conservation hot spots. While the local habitats contain a profusion of endemic species, these have been decimated in the last 40 years by logging. More than 90% of the region's forests have been logged, causing an estimated loss of over half of the plant and animal species. Serious erosion, forest fragments, climate change, and continued human mismanagement threaten the remaining species. The ecological importance of the remaining forests led to the establishment of several nongovernmental organizations, which strive to assist the people of the region to attain a sustainable, self-sufficient future.

What Works

Engaging multiple aspects of community development in the same project leads to increased credibility and success.

Cultural pride, education, environmental health, agriculture, handicrafts, eco-tourism, and civil infrastructure are among the elements that may be pursued in any one village.

A strong element of education, whether adult education through workshops or youth education through school projects, helps ensure a sustainable program.

Villages are invited to participate in a process that they help lead; they are not forced to accept outside intervention.

Maintaining open lines of communication is essential to encouraging community participation.

The region has been inhabited for thousands of years, particularly in the rich, alluvial flood plain of the lower mountains. Earlier people farmed and fished with a complex system of cooperative land ownership. They believed that the forests were living beings, even though they used wood for structures and fuel.

When timber and oil resources were extracted from the region at the turn of the century, the inhabitants were enticed into a cash-based existence. As the oil fields ran dry, layoffs forced a migration to nearby cities for work. A penetrating network of roads to facilitate timber harvest put more of the region at risk. Prolonged droughts and erosion caused the desert to creep farther into the once-forested area.

The Project

The fundamental approach of Fundación Pro-Pueblo and the other nongovernmental organizations is to work with the local people to strengthen their own democratic processes and to safeguard their heritage. The organizations are coordinating their efforts, while extension agents and democratically elected health, ecological, forestry, and home-garden committees have been instrumental in providing communities with activity proposals.

Pro-Pueblo assists communities to improve their standard of living while caring for the environment. In this approach, caring for the environment begins inside people's homes and extends into the hills that surround their villages. Pro-Pueblo emphasizes workshops that equip individuals with practical knowledge, and uses the family unit as a key factor in the change process. Whenever possible, the workshops draw on the experience of the participants. Children are a key component to a long-term educational process and are encouraged to join in weeding the vegetable garden, helping with handicrafts, or recycling garbage. Weekly radio programs and a monthly newsletter provide outlets for people to update other villages about their projects and to build community spirit.

The Results

Only by providing viable alternatives is it possible to convince people living on the edge of existence to extend their few resources and replant, or not to cut the forest. After several years of effort, local people are beginning to see that they can do something. The new understanding of how the environment is integral to their lives complements the tradition of their ancestors. Those who can become self-sufficient will begin to transform their problems into solutions, and will be proud custodians of a corner of the planet that will remain intact for generations to come.

Environmental Education for Tanzania: A Practical Success Story

Mary Shuma
World Wide Fund for Nature (WWF)
Dar Es Salaam, Tanzania

What Works

When a program enables people to carry out their own ideas, they are empowered.

Providing initial ideas and support enables people to take action.

Schools are used as an organizing and changing force in a community.

The Tanzania Environmental Education Programme (TEEP) is a World Wide Fund for Nature (WWF) program designed to enable people to take active and well-informed roles in environmental decisions and actions. The program is implemented in schools, community, media, professional groups, and religious groups.

The Project

One of TEEPs major activities is organizing awareness seminars for primary school teachers, district education officers, and school inspectors. The seminars are designed to increase teachers' awareness of the importance and multidisciplinary nature of environmental issues. Through the seminars, teachers explore ways to introduce environmental education into every school subject. Participants are expected to organize similar seminars for their colleagues.

The Results

When teachers and school inspectors carry their ideas back to other teachers, a variety of results occur. In Morogoro, for example, two primary school teachers started a School Greening Program. This program involves planting grass and trees, establishing tree nurseries, controlling soil erosion, planting a school garden, and digging fish ponds. The involvement of other teachers, school children, and community members makes the program very successful. At Kiroka Primary School, large blocks of bare ground near the school have been planted with grass and trees, and surplus seedlings from the Women's Forestry Group are given to students to plant at home. Several fish ponds produce fish for sale, with proceeds going to the school fund.

Other teachers are working with an alternative to charcoal, known as vegetable charcoal or *Mkaa wa Majani* in Kiswahili. When certain plants (*Corchorus tridens* and grasses) are crushed and boiled, the resulting paste and potash can be used to bind together soil particles, ash from burned rubbish, and water. Small balls are dried in the shade for five days and then they are ready to burn. Children like to make the charcoal, since it is so much like playing in mud.

Ecocultural Tourism in Lombok, Indonesia

Rocky Rohwedder
Sonoma State University
California, United States

In Indonesia, tourism strongly influences small communities and their environments. This project involves students, communities, and nongovernmental organizations in creating alternative tourism strategies that advocate community-based sustainable development, environmental protection and education, and cross-cultural understanding.

The Situation

The Center for Indonesian Studies (CIS) is a nonprofit organization that operates cross-cultural collaborations in grassroots environmental and community projects on the islands of Bali and Lombok, Indonesia. In particular, CIS addresses social, environmental, and cultural problems created by tourism.

In parts of Indonesia, tourism has eroded social and cultural values, has made the local economy dependent on its revenues, and has damaged the

What Works

Participatory Rural Appraisal (PRA) techniques can be used to involve community members in defining a project; these techniques provide insight into the community's socio-environmental problems and needs, and into the relationship between development and society.

After conducting a PRA, tourism strategies the community can develop were identified that preserve important socio-cultural traditions and that provide income-generating opportunities.

Insightful planning, sensitive preparation, and the involvement of community members result in tourism models that are fruitful for indigenous people.

Personal relationships help to establish mutual respect and trust between outside researchers and village members; this respect and trust may be more critical to a successful program than the best of plans or intentions.

communities' political control over their villages. However, the type of tourism—either mass tourism or ecologically and culturally sensitive tourism—greatly defines the type of development that can occur. Tourism can bring positive development, instilling pride in indigenous customs, prompting the protection of ecologically sensitive areas through parks and conservation activities, and boosting the local economy. Where tourism is a positive force, the host community defines its own needs, terms, and benefits for tourism in its region.

The Project

The Rinjani Eco-Development Project is a long-term collaborative effort between several nongovernmental organizations and the community of Senaru. Located on the island of Lombok, Senaru is a village on the slopes of Mt. Rinjani, which is the nation's second highest volcano and one of Indonesia's three major sacred mountains. The Rinjani National Park's winding trails, natural beauty, and phenomenal views attract many climbers to the area.

Specific activities of the Rinjani Eco-Development Project vary from year to year. Recently, student participants conducted surveys of village hamlets; performed preliminary environmental impact assessments; surveyed local tourism patterns; gathered information about the communities' needs with regard to women, water, and health care; and interviewed local guides and other community members. As a result, the project produced a tourist guidebook for those visiting the village and climbing Mt. Rinjani, promoting cross-cultural understanding and supporting indigenous entrepreneurs. Villagers have been given training in language skills, business management, and environmental education. The project also established sustainable eco-villages, hamlets that have integrated environmentally friendly technologies with traditional beliefs in the areas of waste management, food production and processing, and energy production. On a rotating basis, the eco-villages serve as homestays for ecotourists. A women's cooperative runs a restaurant for visiting tourists, where they receive a cultural orientation and meals prior to their hike up Mt. Rinjani.

The Results

Participants contribute to a project that is important, benefits the community, and helps them gain valuable research skills. The project activities have promoted cross-cultural understanding within a context of traditional socio-cultural values and have supported indigenous entrepreneurship. Eco-cultural tourism empowers indigenous communities to maintain their culture and their environment by ensuring that neither be damaged or turned into a commodity for the sake of tourism .

2 CREATING CHANGE IN SCHOOL SYSTEMS

When a formal education system accepts and embraces environmental education, a nation moves several steps closer to environmental solutions. In the following activities, Ministries of Education use a variety of strategies to increase their citizens' environmental literacy.

Training Key Education Personnel in Environmental Education in India

Abdul Ghafoor Ghaznawi
Asian Institute of Environmental Education
Islamabad, Pakistan

What Works

Strong emphasis should be placed on incorporating environmental education into national education policies to ensure a legislative basis for, and continuous development of, environmental education.

Training education decision makers is fundamental to the development of environmental education policy at the national level.

Training education decision makers in environmental education is best done through a variety of methods, including short-term seminars and workshops, implementing pilot projects, adapting documents, and preparing international environmental education documents.

Environmental education training should be based in national education institutions that have the responsibility, capacity, commitment, and interest for educational change at the national level. In this way, the actions of the decision makers have a multiplier effect throughout the nation.

The United Nations Education, Scientific, and Cultural Organization (UNESCO) helped to develop environmental education (EE) in India by working with two national education institutions to train education decision makers in environmental education methods and approaches. This strategy led to India incorporating environmental education into its 1986 National Policy on Education.

The Situation

In 1976, UNESCO decided to make India a special focal point for environmental education development. It is a large, populated nation with a variety of environmental concerns. An inexpensive plan was designed that would involve two national education institutions; their employees would be trained in environmental education and would support educational change throughout India. Both institutions, the National Council of Educational Research and Training (NCERT) and the National

Institute of Educational Planning and Administration (NIEPA), were seeking educational innovations in their respective fields.

The development of environmental education at the national level is a very slow process, especially in countries with a centralized education system like India. Before environmental education could be developed, teacher educators, curriculum developers, and education planners first had to recognize a need for it. This need was promoted through training activities. The trainees were then involved in making decisions about environmental education, such as how to address its political aspect as a tool to empower citizens, what its legislative status should be in the national education policy, and how it should be funded.

The Project

A series of training programs was designed to provide relevant and convincing environmental education activities to NCERT and NIEPA staff. Initially, a pilot project for primary schools was organized by NCERT with the support of UNESCO. The major task was to develop a prototype environmental education module for primary schools that could be studied for possible adaptation at the state level throughout India. Once the module was prepared and tested, NCERT convened a three-day workshop for teachers from each region of India. NCERT also prepared an international teacher training module for pre-service social science teachers, which was released in an international workshop hosted by NCERT.

In 1985, the National Policy on Education of India came under revision and renewal, with NIEPA being partly responsible for the legislative renewal. In order to bring environmental education to the forefront, UNESCO invited NIEPA to prepare and organize a consultative meeting that would provide a holistic look at incorporating environmental education into the educational system by focusing on the training of curriculum developers, teacher educators, and educational planners. At the meeting, the need for the national education policy to include environmental education was emphasized. The message was well taken and well implemented. In 1986, India announced its new National Policy on Education, which considers environmental education as an integral part of the educational system for all types and levels of education.

The Results

The adoption of a national policy that included environmental education was a major achievement for the Indian education decision makers and a major contribution by UNESCO. The involvement of Indian education leaders continues to provide the international environmental education community with materials, conferences, and opportunities to report and exchange important lessons.

A Participatory Process for the Integration of Environmental Education into the Primary School Curriculum in Brazil

Lou Ann Dietz and Vera Rodrigues
WWF-US and WWF-Brazil
United States and Brazil

What Works

An effective guidebook can be written when key partners represent different geographic regions, educational content, and institutions.

Strong local partnerships may be more important than financial resources to ensure continuity; participation in the design of a program strengthens the commitment of partners.

Clear, agreed-upon objectives guarantee quality and effectiveness, and ensure that the project can be evaluated and supported regardless of changing political agendas.

A nongovernmental organization with technical credibility brings continuity and flexibility to a partnership with government agencies.

The coordination of a long-term participatory process requires strategic thinking, leadership, and an intimate knowledge of the realities and institutions at every stage of the development and implementation process.

In a national effort to institutionalize environmental education in Brazilian primary schools, key members of the environmental education community were asked to participate in developing a teaching guide and teacher training courses.

The Situation

The 1988 Brazilian Constitution requires environmental education at all levels of formal education. In spite of successful initiatives in some parts of the country, this policy has not been implemented at the national level. The principal barriers to environmental education are inadequate training for teachers and a lack of resources. In Brazil, 91% of the 1.3 million teachers are women, and the average teacher salary is below Brazil's minimum wage. Most of the teachers (59%) have just a high school education, and 17% of them have just an eighth grade education. Only 63% of the teachers have books, and most teachers limit their teaching methods to lectures with the blackboard.

Despite the barriers, environmental education does occur in a variety of contexts and through various institutions where professional educators care deeply about it. The challenge for this project was to involve these key professionals and institutions in an effective partnership that would create a useful product.

The Project

The project was funded by World Wildlife Fund-US (WWF-US), World Wide Fund for Nature-Brazil (WWF-Brazil) and the United Kingdom Department for International Development. In 1995, the project began by building a partnership among environmental education professionals, government agencies, and nongovernmental organizations to develop ways to integrate environmental education into daily teaching practices in Brazil. All partners made a long-term commitment to the process and supported WWF as the project coordinator.

The project focused on teacher training and curriculum development for grades 1-4. The partners participated in the process in an ongoing way: agreeing on the overall guidelines and objectives for the project, and planning, developing, and testing the materials. The group agreed that the best teaching strategies would encourage teachers to discover their surroundings, participate actively in the identification and solution of problems, research students' reality, establish links with the local community, and build new concepts about their work.

A steering committee negotiated the project design, structure, and objectives for a teacher guidebook through a series of interactive workshops. A professional writer was hired to participate in all of the workshops and to transform the committee's mandate into a product that was thoroughly discussed and reviewed by the committee. The book was then pilot-tested in workshops and reviewed by technical experts. The guidebook is intended to help teachers understand environmental education and to stimulate teachers to integrate teaching about the environment into all disciplines.

The Results

Five thousand copies of the guidebook will be printed and distributed through teacher training courses throughout the country. Partnerships have been developed with universities, agencies, and nongovernmental organizations to conduct the course in six regions over the following year.

Environmental Education in the Senegalese School System

Mamadou Diaw
United States Peace Corps/Senegal
Dakar, Senegal

The United States Peace Corps in Senegal is working closely with the Ministry of National Education to incorporate environmental education into the official curriculum. Peace Corps volunteers conduct workshops on local environmental topics, and then help to design a local environmental education curriculum.

The Situation

Senegal is facing recurrent droughts and progressive desertification. Most reforestation projects funded by international donors have focused on technical solutions, not on the causes of the problem. As a result, these projects have failed to improve the environmental situation. In 1990, Senegal adopted environmental education as a means to tackle desertification by addressing people's awareness, knowledge, and behaviors. Despite the political will to achieve environmental education, progress has been slow. This project provides grassroots support to the Ministry of National Education through Peace Corps volunteers.

The Project

In this project, Peace Corps volunteers work with teachers and school inspectors to develop and test environmental education curricula focusing on local environmental problems. The project is designed to last six years and to target nine regions of Senegal, including 150 rural primary schools and their surrounding communities.

The strategy is to develop for each District School an environmental education curriculum, based on local environmental problems, that increases students' environmental awareness. The volunteers work in collaboration with the school inspectors, local foresters, and other environmental organizations to assess the teachers' environmental knowledge and training needs. Volunteers help to organize local workshops, where environmental and pedagogical topics are explored and the local curriculum is designed. Each curriculum is complemented by school projects, animation activities with environmental education bulletins, and outdoor activities.

In addition to increasing students' environmental awareness, the project is increasing the ability of the participating schools to design their own curricula It also promotes environmental awareness among the community through information and publicity campaigns, and reinforces the capacity of the Ministry to coordinate and monitor environmental education projects.

The Results

After three years, 223 teachers have been trained in environmental education. Three local curricula have been developed and tested, and three Districts have completed their programs. The curricula, because they are focused on local environmental problems, become relevant and interesting to the rural students. Many teachers are conducting environmental awareness activities in their classrooms. The participatory approach to this project also resulted in the creation of a nationwide network of teachers and school inspectors who are extremely committed to environmental education, and a new national curriculum is being developed by the Ministry.

Teachers and school inspectors had been somewhat reluctant to add another topic to their already full schedules. By placing Peace Corps volunteers in the schools, the project helped ease the burden and demonstrate how environmental education can be infused into other subjects. It has been difficult to involve the communities because the project targets students. Without additional funding, schools have been unable to initiate community projects.

"Ecologizing" Education in Russia

Margarita Arutiunian
Khabarovsk Regional Institute for Teacher Training and
Qualification
Khabarovsk, Russia

What Works

Opening the lines of communication between teachers and students changes the nature of their interaction: rather than teachers being the authoritative provider of information, teachers respect student contributions to an investigation of information.

Encouraging an interactive, human-based approach to teacher training and education helps to transform education.

Radio broadcasts about environmental education for children raise public awareness of its importance.

Environmental education is integrated into stories, art, music, and drama.

The ecologization of education reflects a process of transformation of the Russian education system to include, among other things, a thematic integration of disciplines. A variety of programs in Russia's Far East are dedicated to the cultivation of a thoughtful and informed attitude toward nature.

The Situation

The traditional method of instruction is challenged by this program through an introduction of a variety of theories, including Deep Ecology and the equality of all beings. By investigating ways to promote a regional emphasis on environmental education, this program encourages teachers to increase their environmental education efforts and to foster in young children a compassion for the environment . The development of strong teacher-student relations is one way educators can encourage the transition from absolute scientism and Marxism-Leninism to humanism and democracy.

The Project

One project of the Institute asks high school students about the behavior of teachers toward students. Questionnaires are used to help teachers re-evaluate their own teaching style and move away from the static lecture-based format. Seating patterns and positions are open to experimentation as teachers question the need to stay at the head of the classroom or require students to stand when speaking. An experimental school (No. 63) enables the Institute to test these teaching methods and techniques.

At several other schools and youth centers, additional teaching methods are applied and tested. At the children's art studio (*Skazochek*), for example, environmental education is integrated into art, music, dance, and other creative activities. At an environmental center (*Rodnicheck*), students are involved in environmental discovery and experiments during and after school.

A series of radio programs on environmental education for children has recently been launched. When the general understanding of environmental education and its importance is increased, the ecologization of education will occur on a larger scale.

The lack of support materials for teaching, research, outreach, training, and seminars is a serious constraint to expanding environmental education efforts. Additional constraints include the lack of current environmental information, lack of access to libraries and the Internet, lack of exchange opportunities, and some educators resistance to change. The creative potential of the region's educators, their love for the children, their ability to overcome hardship, and their constant hope for positive change will indeed bring fundamental changes in education and in the environment for future generations.

(Translation by Miranda Lutyens)

Environmental Curriculum Development in Elementary Schools in Bulgaria

Veleslava Tzakova
This is My Environment (TIME) Foundation
Sofia, Bulgaria

A two-year, community-based, participatory process in Bulgaria resulted in the development of an interdisciplinary environmental education curriculum, a manual of interactive lessons, and the professional development of over 30 teachers.

The Project

The TIME Foundation, with support from the United States Information Agency and the Institute for Sustainable Communities (ISC), created a process to involve teachers and community members in developing environmental education methods and materials for primary grades. An initial organizing meeting with organizers, relevant ministries, and local nongovernmental organizations established support and criteria for the project.

TIME and ISC jointly led a seminar to introduce interactive environmental education teaching methods to primary grade teachers in two communities. These teachers, in working groups,

What Works

An organizing meeting attended by all relevant parties (in this case, Ministries of Education, Science and Technology, Environment, and Health; Sofia University, and NGOs) is critical for establishing support and criteria for the project.

Calling on an expert (in this case, a professor from the National In-Service Teacher Training Center) ensures the quality of products.

Initial site visits help to motivate teachers to accept the ideas and goals of environmental education, and exchanges with teachers in other communities help to continue this excitement and motivation.

An interdisciplinary approach is truly helpful in the classroom.

developed supplementary curriculum materials and organized classes to share these methods with other colleagues.

One year after the initial organizing meeting, a workshop allowed teachers from the two pilot communities to share their experiences and to discuss a manual that would record their efforts. Teachers from four other communities also attended the workshop to learn more about environmental education. For three months after the workshop, teachers revised their ideas and a professor from the Teachers Institute edited the curriculum materials.

The Results

As a result of the project, two manuals were produced. *Curriculum for Integrated Environmental Education* shows how environmental education can be infused into each primary grade subject and describes possible environmental activities. *Manual for Teachers* contains 120 interactive lessons for all subject areas and was approved for distribution by the Higher Experts Council of the Ministry of Education.

The current challenges are to implement the curriculum through a nation-wide teacher training program and to expand the program to include more grade levels and new communities. The two groups of teachers will remain active in the program, demonstrating their interactive lessons at teacher workshops and motivating other teachers to participate in the expansion process.

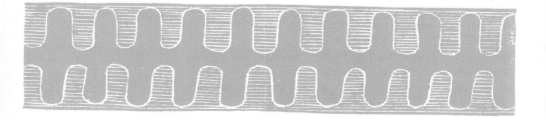

"Old Sable:" A Russian-American Environmental Education Project

Linda Rhines and Michael Brody
Institute for Sustainable Communities and Montana State University
United States

With funding from the United States Environmental Protection Agency, the Institute for Sustainable Communities worked in partnership with the Nizhnii Tagil Pedagogical Institute to develop community-based environmental education for high school students in Nizhni Tagil, Russia. The project focused on teacher training, developing interactive curricula, and increasing public awareness of environmental issues.

The Situation

Nizhni Tagil is a city of 440,000 people in the southern Ural Mountains formerly closed to foreigners. The city was designated one of Russia's first environmental emergency zones because of industrial pollution from metallurgy and chemical industries. The city has one of the highest rates of lung and stomach cancers in the Russian Federation. Only four percent of the community's children are considered healthy, and one of every eight children dies between the ages of four and seven. The Nizhnii

What Works

Needs assessment and pre-project planning are essential to understand the situation, and to help the partners collaboratively define project goals.

Involving teachers in curriculum development can produce positive, though unexpected, results; for example, school teachers and Pedagogical Institute professors now have better working relationships.

American staff with Russian language skills and a United States study tour help to develop a working relationship and to build rapport.

In a successful project, all partners play an important role; even if one partner is more powerful, joint decisions about partners' roles should be made so that all partners agree to their tasks and have a voice in the plan.

Tagil Environmental Education Project (titled "Old Sable" for the city's namesake) was part of a larger, multi-component project in the city, jointly managed by the Institute for Sustainable Communities and the Nizhni Tagil Pedagogical Institute from 1994 to 1996. The project was implemented during a difficult period of rapid political, economic, and social change.

The Project

Focusing on high school biology, the project helped teachers, teacher trainers, and members of the community discover how they could cultivate environmental stewardship in young people. The project included a community-based curriculum development effort that involved government, teachers, college faculty, nonformal educators, business people, and parents. The resulting new environmental education curricula were also tested in local schools. A teacher training component included four on-site training workshops, giving teachers new methods and resources for teaching core subjects while involving students in the natural world and in local environmental issues. The project also helped develop a new pre-service teacher training course at the Pedagogical Institute. An international conference highlighted the results of the project, with participants from 18 cities in the Ural region working to develop a framework for expanding the curriculum project to grades K-12.

The Results

The project catalyzed the city administration to make environmental education a top priority and to provide financial support for continuing the environmental education program. Legislation enacted by Nizhni Tagil's mayor put environmental education in the required curriculum for all 66 high schools. Teacher education programs were developed by the Pedagogical Institute. New environmental education courses were created in all of the city's high schools. The number of workshops held to distribute materials and train teachers had to be increased to accommodate the broad interest. An Ecology Teachers Association was formed and the project partners experienced opportunities to increase cooperation and communication.

3 USING MASS MEDIA

Electronic media can act as a key to catalyzing large numbers of citizens with information about environmental issues. Training for journalists and other personnel in the media world and the careful analysis of existing knowledge and behaviors are important components in developing effective media campaigns.

Formative Research Shapes an Environmental Campaign in Eygpt

Orlando Hernández
GreenCOM Project
Washington DC, United States

In developing a water-scarcity awareness campaign in Egypt, farmers from three regions of the country were consulted about their knowledge, beliefs, and practices related to irrigation water.

The Situation

Thanks to the Nile River, Egypt has had an abundance of water for centuries. With the construction of the Aswan High Dam, however, Egypt agreed to share the Nile River water with neighboring countries. Through an established agreement, Egypt can release no more than 55.5 billion cubic meters from the High Dam per year. Within the past 10 years, Egypt has moved from having a water surplus to a water deficit. In 1996, for example, Egypt needed approximately 63 billion cubic meters, the difference being made up by reusing water. The Ministry of Public Works and Water Resources (MPWWR) in Egypt is interested in making farmers aware of the country's

What Works

Getting acquainted with the target audience helps technicians design better environmental communication programs.

Technicians directly participating in collecting and analyzing data about the target audience become stronger researchers, gain irreplaceable first-hand experience with issues worrying farmers, and develop a two-way communication with the farmers.

Reinforcing positive actions that the target audience is already taking increases the effectiveness of the campaign.

Formative research helps to identify barriers to and incentives for desired behaviors.

Since men and women often have different roles and perspectives in environmental issues, both are consulted to determine if different messages should be developed.

water-scarcity problems, and requested assistance from the GreenCOM Project (funded by the United States Agency for International Development) to develop a communication campaign to meet that objective.

The Project

Staff members from the Water Communication Unit of the MPWWR attended a training course where they learned how to interview people and how to conduct focus groups. They then worked in three Nile River communities to record impressions and collect feedback from farmers about the campaign messages. While MPWWR technicians had an idea for the campaign prior to the research, as a result of the research some topics were added or dropped, creating a very different campaign. The experience reinforced the need to consult with audiences for environmental education and communication programs to identify appropriate content and messages.

The Results

As a result of the research, the focus of the campaign changed to recognize and reinforce the ways farmers already manage water efficiently. The campaign also stressed the importance of water conservation practices to ensure present and future family food needs. Neither of these topics was originally considered by technicians. The research also allowed campaign designers to drop references to water scarcity's role in armed conflicts and to the Egyptian public sector's water conservation efforts. Religious overtones and the relationship of water scarcity to population growth were topics that were retained.

The Environmental Journalist Seminar: A Communications Tool for Conservation

Patricia B. Kelly
Conservation International
Washington DC, United States

What Works

Journalists play a key role in national environmental strategies by communicating understandable information to many different people in a nation.

Seminars for environmental journalists are developed with local partners to help educate journalists about environmental issues and to motivate them to increase environmental coverage.

Communication coordinators working with successful environmental projects disperse information about their projects to journalists through e-mail, local field trips, and traveling teams.

Networks of journalists and partnerships with international organizations (such as the International Federation of Environmental Journalists) help improve professional skills.

The media perform an important function in conservation efforts. Conservation International (CI) has been involved in training and empowering journalists to report on environmental issues and successful environmental projects in the hope that public opinion and policy may be shaped to enhance conservation goals.

The Situation

In the summer of 1987, CI pioneered a new strategy in environmental conservation: a debt-for-nature swap. The government of Bolivia agreed to protect 3 million acres of tropical forest in exchange for the cancellation of $2 million in international debt. The innovative deal was announced at the Bolivian embassy in a major news conference and launched a flurry of news stories.

Six months later, however, conservationists realized that no one in Bolivia understood the treaty and what it meant. The policy could not be implemented without policy makers and reserve neighbors understanding it. Rather than coordinating its own communication strategy, CI worked with LIDEMA (a coordinating nongovernmental organization for Bolivian environmental organizations) and the National Association of Bolivian Journalists to arrange a seminar for journalists from throughout the country. Over three days, the journalists learned about environmental issues, discussed their needs, and engaged in debate. They decided to form their own group and to tap LIDEMA for information and data.

The Project

CI has extended this seminar model, providing professional development for would-be environmental journalists throughout the tropics. In almost every case, CI has learned that journalists in tropical countries want to do a better job covering serious environmental issues. Almost uniformly, they lack access to information and environmental data, story ideas, and a feeling of connectedness to other environmental journalists in the region. CI's seminars begin to solve these problems by building networks between countries, providing environmental information, hosting field trips to deforestation sites, and showing how the media can play a role in shaping environmental policy.

The Results

The environmental journalist seminars, and the resulting networks of journalists, have been successful in increasing the media role in conservation efforts. In one example, after a South-North Journalist Exchange in British Columbia, journalists from Brazil, Mexico, Canada, and the United States wrote stories on local logging practices. Amid a spate of bad press, policy makers in British Columbia reduced their deforestation goals. In another example, a group formed out of a similar seminar in Guyana, the Association of Guyanese Environmental Media, was awarded a grant from the W. Alton Jones Foundation to develop its professional group.

Promoting Conservation Awareness through Electronic Media

Katarina Panji
World Wide Fund for Nature-Indonesia
Jakarta, Indonesia

World Wide Fund for Nature in Indonesia (WWF-I) worked with television and radio producers to broadcast existing programs and to create new ones that increase public awareness of conservation issues in Indonesia.

The Situation

Indonesia is an island nation and the fourth most populous country in the world. Nearly 10% of its land area is protected in conservation areas, but the public has not been very aware of these areas. One government-owned and five privately owned television stations broadcast programs to the major population areas, and the islands have over 700 radio stations. This project used these electronic media to increase public awareness of environmental and conservation issues and to generate interest for protection.

What Works

Electronic media raise public awareness of conservation issues.

Tapes and other materials are provided so that radio and TV stations can test a new program direction with little commitment of their own resources.

Public interest and success with initial materials spawn commitment from stations to produce their own programs, features, and talk shows.

Talk show formats are particularly effective at generating interest and communicating a message.

Commercial stations are often less likely to donate air time to public service announcements, but a strong partnership and demonstrated interest can win their cooperation.

Locally produced television programs are more effective and more interesting than internationally produced programs.

The Project

In 1994, WWF-I began producing short radio bulletins for distribution to over 600 radio stations throughout the nation. Along with tapes, WWF-I provides fact sheets and background information for additional radio scripting. The interest in these bulletins has grown to include a weekly radio talk show aimed at listeners who are 25-30 years old. The talk show format consists of guest speakers and calls from listeners, and covers a variety of issues, such as pollution and wildlife trade. In a cooperative arrangement, one radio station provides a crew, producer, and production costs, and WWF-I provides a staff person to coordinate the show. WWF-I also offers field staff and technical expertise when the shows revolve around local environmental issues. Local nongovernmental organizations are also involved in locally broadcast talk shows.

Initially, television stations were reluctant to use commercial time to broadcast short environmental messages. After airing several feature programs on environmental issues, however, they realized the strong public interest and the newsworthiness of conservation issues.

The Results

The program generated public interest around several important conservation themes. Even more importantly, the media became interested in producing their own programs and covering environmental issues. The largest television station is very cooperative, and its commitment stimulates other partnerships. Other nongovernmental organizations are also now involved in providing technical assistance for radio programs that are broadcast in their regions. A series of important partnerships has been established connecting the environmental community with the broadcast media (both private and government) in Indonesia.

Educational Documentaries as the Centerpiece of Informational Campaigns

Haroldo Castro
Conservation International
Washington DC, United States

Conservation International (CI) uses television documentaries in its information campaigns because they convey powerful conservation messages and provide a way to hook the media. In Brazil's Pantanal and in Tambopata, Peru, documentaries helped to bring positive results to CI's conservation efforts.

The Situation

CI builds public awareness about the importance of biological diversity and the actions needed to conserve it in biodiversity-rich countries. In most areas, development pressures from population and agriculture are reducing native habitat. Information about alternatives to the destruction of natural resources and the value of their preservation is critical.

To capture the attention and to change the attitudes of the national and regional audiences, CI designs intensive media campaigns that create arenas for public discussions. Ultimately, these efforts are intended to influence national policymakers who make the crucial decisions on the future of threatened ecosystems. CI uses television

What Works

Due to the overwhelming importance of television in much of the world, video products are extremely effective information tools.

Using appropriate cultural and national values allows the message to be heard and assimilated.

Media events help to launch broadcast-quality television documentaries and create increased publicity.

Production of a high-quality video product on a controversial subject helps insure broadcast and support from the private sector and government agencies.

Raising the awareness and level of information of the general public helps to exert pressure on decision makers for responsible conservation actions.

documentaries as the centerpiece of information campaigns. Launching a documentary is news. By making it a media event announced and discussed in the press, CI can, in turn, increase television viewing. CI also distributes videotapes to nongovernmental organizations and teachers to expand a documentary's impact even more.

The Projects

The Pantanal is the world's largest freshwater wetland and a fertile haven for wildlife. Its existence is dependent upon the seasonal flooding of the Paraguay River in Brazil. A controversial international development project, Hydrovia, would change the natural flow and design of the river and would impact the flooding system. CI created an informational video to promote public discussion based on interviews with scientists, conservationists, cattle ranchers, politicians, indigenous people, and business leaders. During the video's production, the controversy began to turn toward a conservation solution. Thus, a Brazilian official stated he was making a commitment to leave the river as it is.

CI conducted another project in Tambopata, in the Peruvian Amazon—one of the most biologically diverse regions on Earth and a top global conservation priority. Although it was declared a Reserved Zone, uncontrolled development continued to threaten the region. CI designed a national information campaign to relay the urgency of establishing the area as a national park. In order to influence decision-makers, CI created *Return to Tambopata*, a 28-minute documentary. Prominent Peruvian and international corporate executives, key political players, diplomats, and congressmen attended the premier of the documentary in Lima. Over 30 articles were published about the documentary in the Peruvian press. After it aired nationally on prime-time television, a street survey showed that 69% of the public had been directly touched by the campaign.

The Results

In Brazil, a wide showing of the documentary *Voices of the Pantanal* in December 1995 in the Pantanal region, with full-page newspaper stories led to public support for the Pantanal. Universities, schools, and nongovernmental organizations still show the video and use the accompanying educators' booklet. The publicity is making any change from the leave-the-river-as-it-is policy much more difficult. Years later, Hydrovia has not yet been implemented.

In Peru, the documentary *Return to Tambopata* and its campaign launched in February 1996 was key to triggering the final political decision to create a national park. In July 1996, the Peruvian government established the Bahuaja-Sonene National Park, granting permanent protection to 30% of the former Reserved Zone.

"Sëkó:" Mass Media for a National Environmental Ethic in Costa Rica

Guillermo A. Canessa Mora, Luis Fernando Rojas, Osvaldo Valerín
Costa Rica Civic Center
San Jose, Costa Rica

What Works

A broad partnership co-sponsors this major initiative.

Mass media helps to change how a nation thinks about environmental issues.

Costa Rica's national conservation strategy includes a chapter on the role of and actions for the communications sector.

Sëkó (which means "our place" or "our time" in the native language of the Bribri Indians) is a national media project in Costa Rica. It involves the partnership of several agencies and organizations to produce and air a series of one-minute environmental documentaries designed to change Costa Ricans' attitudes toward conservation.

The Situation

Costa Rica answered the challenge of the United Nations conferences in Stockholm (1972) and in Rio de Janeiro (1992) by developing a national conservation strategy known as ECODES (Strategy for Conservation and Sustainable Development of Costa Rica). In keeping with the International Union for the Conservation of Nature and Natural Resources suggestion (1984) that national strategies recognize the important role media can play in the formation of public opinion on conservation,

ECODES includes a chapter on the role of and actions for the communications sector.

The Project

In response to ECODES, the Costa Rica Civic Foundation has launched Sëkó, the Campaign Mass Media for a National Environmental Ethic. The project will involve creating a massive television campaign to change the public's attitudes toward the conservation of Costa Rica's biodiversity and natural resources. The Ministry of Environment and Energy will contribute to the project by providing air time two minutes a day, six days a week, on 12 national channels. The University for Peace, the University of Costa Rica's School of Biology, and the Ministry of Education also support the project.

The television campaign will be developed through a series of one-minute documentaries. These spots will promote sustainable development, environmental ethics, and the principles and values associated with modern ecological culture. The documentaries will explain ecological concepts, describe case studies of successful and unsuccessful ventures, demonstrate activities, honor anonymous ecological heroes, and show national protected areas. The second phase of the project will produce at least four major documentaries for use in the broadcast media.

The Results

The expected result of this project is that it will motivate the public to support ecologically sustainable behaviors. The project will be evaluated internally by exploring accomplishments and the quality of the relationships that have been formed, and externally by measuring impacts and influences.

4 FOSTERING ENVIROMENTAL POLICY

Environmental education and communication
activities can help support, formulate, and convey
national environmental policies. It is vital
that citizens become more aware of important
environmental legislation, and in some cases
projects are designed to inform policy makers
of citizen opinions.

Combatting Desertification in Pakistan with Environmental Communication Strategies

Syed Jamil Hasan Kazmi
SCOPE
Karachi, Pakistan

Sand and gravel mining in the Malir Valley of Pakistan has seriously altered the ecosystem. Through a scientific study, public hearings, and meetings with government officials, the Society for Conservation and Protection of Environment (SCOPE) convinced the government to enforce a regulation against sand and gravel mining.

The Situation

In Pakistan's Malir Valley, the seasonal Malir River carries rainwater to the Arabian Sea. Coarse sand and gravel along the river bottom slow the water and allow it to replenish the groundwater aquifer. For centuries, a thriving agricultural community in the valley depended on groundwater for irrigation. Recently, however, excessive sand mining along the river bed exposed the bedrock and resulted in water scarcity and desertification in the valley. Unfortunately, a government prohibition against sand and gravel mining in the Malir Valley was too

What Works

Scientific data help to form a solid foundation for action.

Involving scientific institutions helps ensure that solid data are collected.

In the beginning stages of a project, careful and strategic presentation of scientific data builds credibility and earns the trust of local people, the media, and the government.

Coordinating efforts among stakeholders, nongovernmental organizations, the university, and the municipal government helps create a stronger position.

Projects that begin with data collection and use public advocacy to affect government changes often take years to complete, and may cost more than short-term projects.

Identifying and mobilizing the sympathetic people in government will contribute to the success of a project.

weak to be effective: It was not comprehensive and the penalty was not enough of a deterrent. As a result, bribery was commonly used by sand lifters to ensure their illegal activity. SCOPE began tackling this problem in 1992.

The Project

SCOPE began by collecting scientific data about the sand, gravel, water, river, and farming situation, focusing on the rate and impacts of sand and gravel mining. The results of its investigations were announced through press releases to the general public and in consultation meetings with policy makers. SCOPE discovered that mining contributed to lowering the water table, loss of top soil, erosion, salt water intrusion, excessive flooding, reduction in biodiversity, unemployment, and increased poverty. For example, investigations revealed that the water table had fallen from 15 feet in 1960 to more than 200 feet below the surface in 1990. These results, along with two public hearings, helped to establish credibility for SCOPE.

The Results

Faced with such powerful information and with the original intent of the government statement against sand and gravel excavation, district authorities were compelled to take action to halt illegal mining. Now local organizations and businesses help monitor the mining operations by notifying SCOPE or the newspapers of violations. The government has sanctioned three medium-scale irrigation projects in the area to increase groundwater levels. The quantity of excavated sand was reduced to 2% of the quantity before SCOPE's involvement.

SCOPE is continuing efforts to sustain agriculture in the Malir Valley by coordinating efforts among stakeholders, such as nongovernmental organizations, the university, farmers, and local government. SCOPE is seeking more comprehensive and specific legislation to ensure the protection of the Malir Valley and is also promoting participatory groundwater management systems and water conservation irrigation techniques.

Advocacy for the Reform of Forest Management Policy in the Philippines

Chris Seubert
Global Vision, Inc.
Silver Spring, United States

The Natural Resources Management Project (NRMP) provides technical assistance through the Philippines Department of Environment and Natural Resources. NRMP is working at two different levels toward forest management policy reform: with key policy makers in the national Congress and with local communities to strengthen their advocacy capabilities.

The Situation

Community-Based Forest Management (CBFM) is a strategy aimed at resolving the underlying causes of deforestation—such as uncontrolled access to forest lands and lack of local authority over forest lands—by empowering local communities to manage forests in a sustainable manner. For many years in the Philippines, the Department of Environment and Natural Resources and others concerned about the country's depleting forest resources pushed for revision of the Forestry Code to include CBFM. Such a revision requires legislation passed by Congress and signed by the President.

What Works

NRMP recognizes that lawmakers have local interests, that advocates must target their appeals to those interests, and that advocates must show the issue is supported by constituents.

Journalists with access to politicians can conduct surveys of lawmakers' views on policy reform.

Targeting policy makers who have influence and can push an issue forward is crucial for revising legislation or policy. Establishing positive relationships with these champions and providing them with one-on-one assistance gives them the information and support they need.

Mobilizing local groups helps to support policy reforms.

The Project

NRMP is funded by the United States Agency for International Development; Global Vision, Inc., is responsible for its information, education, and communication component. The project took on the challenge of working toward forest management policy reform. The goals are to work with Congress, local government, and community leaders to achieve passage of a revised Forestry Code centered on the principle of CBFM and to increase local participation in the policy-making process.

At the national level, NRMP conducted a survey to learn the current perceptions of legislators and other leaders on forest management practices and policy by contracting with journalists to conduct the interviews. The survey provided the foundation for understanding the technical and political interplay behind previous forest management efforts, as well as advocacy entry points. Printed materials and videos were developed. Champions were identified who would act as sponsors and advocates for the forest management reform bill both inside and outside of Congress.

At the local level, NRMP worked with CBFM communities to convince their congressional representatives to represent accurately the community interests in the national legislature. This was achieved by mobilizing local district assemblies for CBFM, which created a venue for face-to-face dialogue between constituents and their representatives. NRMP also mobilized the support of local governments and multi-sectoral advocacy organizations; Multi-Sectoral Forest Protection Committees, for example, were already receptive to CBFM policies since they bring together different organizations from civil society, academe, upland communities, media, military, and local government to act as watchdogs against illegal logging.

The Results

NRMP shows that policy advocacy must be directed simultaneously at policy makers and at the grassroots level to be most effective. As a result of the project, Congress has authored and sponsored a bill supporting CBFM. Nine national public hearings on CBFM were sponsored by the House Committee, and recommendations from these public hearings were adopted by the committee. In President Ramos's 1995 State of the Nation Address, he identified the revision of forest management policy as an important issue. At the local level, municipal- and barangay-level resolutions have adopted CBFM.

Conserving Sonoran Coastal Wetlands through Public Involvement and Environmental Education

Mariana Lazcano-Ferrat
Pronatura Sonora
Sonora, Mexico

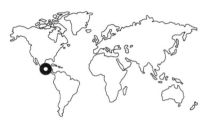

Pronatura Sonora, an environmental nongovernmental organization in the state of Sonora, Mexico, designed a public involvement program for the long-term management of coastal wetlands. The Public Involvement and Education (PIE) program led to a series of successful teacher-led projects in rural areas, covering 11 wetland systems in a coastal area of 540,000 hectares.

The Project

In the first year of the program, 60 representatives from 25 agencies in the region participated in two three-day workshops where, among other tasks, they developed guidelines for involving the public in wetlands planning, management, and decision-making processes. Those guidelines included the following:
- conserve wetlands for and by the people
- recognize community values and reinforce the people's sense of place

What Works

Representatives from many agencies jointly develop guidelines supporting public involvement in wetlands planning, management, and decision-making processes.

The program meets the needs of all the stakeholders; in this case, the Ministry of Education cosponsors teacher workshops, teachers receive professional development credit for attending, and Pronatura gains credibility in the education community.

As educators and respected members of their communities, teachers effectively spread the program to rural regions.

- increase public participation through motivation, awareness, and education
- respect and coordinate conservation initiatives
- integrate community leaders in the program
- reinforce existing programs
- evaluate the results according to criteria established by the community.

The Ministry of Education contributed to the process by offering human resources and the infrastructure to inform citizens and to encourage them to participate. The Ministry also committed to support an extension program suggested by teachers during a workshop.

Through the PIE program, Pronatura Sonora launched a cycle of six workshops for teachers in four communities. Teachers receive information about wetlands and environmental education techniques that enable them to develop action projects such as habitat enhancement. Workshop materials were designed to link wetland management with public action and education. The Ministry of Education cosponsors the workshops, which are evaluated by the Federal Technical Training Committee. The workshops are incorporated into the state training program, which enables teachers to receive salary increases when they reach a certain level of experience.

The Results

Teachers have an excellent multiplier effect; they not only directly teach students, but are also respected community members. Through the initiative of several workshop participants, five teachers were trained to be workshop facilitators. Their instruction included how to share information, design workshops, evaluate materials, and conduct field trips in wetlands. These facilitators have extended the reach of PIE far beyond the initial plan. They are directing community action projects, such as festivals celebrating wetlands, and are coordinating follow-up activities with teachers.

As the PIE program continues, it will incorporate additional suggestions from teachers. The PIE program and the participating agencies plan to produce materials that answer basic questions about wetlands legislation, salt production, fisheries, tourism, and multi-cultural perspectives, and to involve other sectors of the community such as aquaculture technicians, tourism promoters, fishers and farmers.

Stopping Illegal Trafficking of Wildlife in Guatemala

Myriam Monterroso
ARCAS
Peten, Guatemala

Wildlife Rescue and Conservation Association (ARCAS) is a nongovernmental nonprofit organization committed to preserving Guatemalan wildlife and habitat. Its education activities focus on helping Guatemalans recognize the importance of preserving their natural environment.

The Situation

ARCAS was originally formed in 1989 to rescue wild animals confiscated under CITES (the Convention on International Trade in Endangered Species of Wild Fauna and Flora) regulations and has since branched out into ecotourism, habitat preservation, and sustainable community development. Through its work, it became apparent to ARCAS that environmental regulations, wildlife preserves, or monitoring wildlife trafficking could not be effective without education. Environmental education has become a greater component of ARCAS's activities and now comprises about 40% of its programs.

What Works

Interactive, hands-on educational programs, like puppets, slides, clowns, live animals, confiscated animal products, and theater productions, help to involve audiences in the learning process.

When children directly experience touching, smelling, and hearing wild animals, the educational programs have greater impact.

Beach clean-ups and turtle release races help create enthusiasm among students.

Working with teachers in the Peten region makes a broad-based, long-term impact on the education of young people.

In small communities, ARCAS uses an integrated approach to environmental management, combining health, nutrition, food processing, and environmental issues; this helps to build the organization's credibility as a supporter of community development.

The Project

In the region of Peten in northern Guatemala, a Conservation School was built next to ARCAS's Wildlife Rehabilitation Center. Students and teachers visit the school for environmental education experiences and workshops. ARCAS worked with teachers to develop an environmental component for the regional curriculum, which is now approved by authorities and is used throughout the region.

In the town of Hawaii on the Pacific coast, four school hatcheries have been built to give students an opportunity to care for and release sea turtle hatchlings. Local collectors donate eggs, which are buried in the protected hatcheries. Students are involved in releasing the hatchlings.

Building on its successes, ARCAS opened an Environmental Education Office in Guatemala City to coordinate activities and provide programs. Staffed by a variety of personnel and volunteers, the office conducts lectures, plays, and other interactive educational activities in area schools.

The Results

ARCAS staff members have observed a change of attitude in the children and communities toward wildlife, and increased awareness about the problem of illegal trafficking in wildlife. The success of its varied activities has lead ARCAS to plan the purchase of a vehicle for conducting mobile environmental education activities, to expand the education department, to develop more materials, and to establish a library.

5 SUPPLEMENTING FORMAL EDUCATION

Perhaps the majority of environmental education efforts around the world invest in teaching resources, curriculum materials, and training opportunities to enhance school children's understanding of the environment. This small collection of examples indicates the enormous variety such programs offer, as well as the time and effort required for a high quality product.

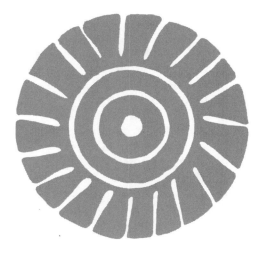

Adapting Environmental Education Materials for Hungary

Andrea Deri and Jamie Watts
United States Peace Corps
Hungary and United States

What Works

Successful adaptations translate words, alter pictures, change instructions, and consider layout to meet the needs of the new audience.

The target audience should have input into the adaptation at several times during the process—the earlier the better—and the needs of the audience should be clearly defined and met.

Collaborative adaptations among several groups help share resources, skills, and distribution channels.

When different pieces of the adaptation are done by different people or organizations, the group needs to work together to design the final product.

The chronic lack of environmental education materials in much of the world leads educators to adapt materials written in the United States, the United Kingdom, Germany, or other developed countries. In two different projects in Hungary, environmental education materials were adapted for local use.

The Situation

Environmental educators typically find that interactive, accurate, and interesting materials are not available for their precise situation. Yet, materials do exist that could be adapted to their particular nation, ecosystem, environmental concern, teaching style, or student level. If done well, the process of adapting materials can be more cost-effective than developing original materials, and may lead to additional development efforts. In Hungary, two independent adaptation efforts highlight how successful projects should be undertaken and the problems that can arise.

The Project

Three organizations (the United States Peace Corps and two nongovernmental organizations involved in environmental education) jointly agreed to produce a Hungarian version of *A Key to Freshwater Macro-Invertebrates*, developed by the Field Studies Council in the United Kingdom. First, volunteers from these organizations roughly translated the document, then asked teachers to comment on it. They discovered that teachers wanted a larger laminated chart for use outdoors and an information sheet for indoor use. Volunteers from all three organizations worked to identify resources for translation, computer layout, expert review, and production. They also shared their distribution lists to reduce dissemination costs. Each organization gained in skills and networking, and two groups were inspired to continue to adapt materials. The Hungarian version of the *Key* was produced economically.

In another example, Hungarian teachers enthusiastically requested a translation of several wall posters produced by United States federal agencies about drinking and surface water. They were attracted to the colorful artwork and the appropriateness of the theme. The adaptation produced a series of pretty, color posters with Hungarian subtitles. However, because the target audience was not defined or consulted, the final product is not very useful. Many of the colorful images are meaningless to Hungarian children, and the translated text still contains American phrases. The cost of producing four-color posters was very high.

The Results

These two efforts had different results. A comparison of the two projects provides these suggestions for others when adapting materials:

Before adaptations are made to existing materials, it may be helpful to define the broad environmental education strategy for the region or nation.

The audience, needs, issues, program implementation, and evaluation need to be clearly defined. Questions include: Who is the audience for the adapted material? How does the audience plan to use the material? With what age level, cultural group, location, or environmental issue will the audience use the material?

Possible materials should be screened for relevance and adaptability. When a draft version of the adaptation is available, the members of the target audience should use and review it. Be sure to make the teaching instructions appropriate, translate jargon or slang, localize the plant and animal examples, and change the images of people, clothing, houses, or landscape to fit the local situation.

Environmental Education for Primary School Teachers in Mexico

Lizbeth Baqueiro
Consejo de Mejoramiento Ambiental
Queretaro, Mexico

What Works

The project is designed to meet a variety of needs from a variety of stakeholders.

Local talent, local resources, and local industries provide support and resources.

The curriculum development project started small, then expanded as the coalition grew.

A small group of professionals worked together to convert a good idea into a successful project.

To promote environmental education in the rural Mexican state of Queretaro, a theoretical and practical teacher training course was designed for primary teachers.

The Situation

Small towns and isolated communities dot the landscape of Queretaro, Mexico. Located in the heart of Mexico's mountains, one-third of this state is neotropical, while another third is neoarctic. Poverty, health problems, erosion, deforestation, and water pollution are commonplace. The native culture is disappearing due to the twin threats of people leaving to work illegally in the United States and the appeal of status-enhancing goods.

There are several barriers to environmental education in Querataro. Teachers with little background in environmental resources tend to avoid the natural science component of the primary curriculum. Even when environmental topics are presented in the curriculum, they are often irrelevant to rural communities. In addition, nonformal environmental education activities throughout Mexico tend to be fragmented because nongovernmental organizations serve their local areas with little strategic planning or coordination with other state or national efforts.

The Project

Consejo de Mejoramiento Ambiental is a group of communicators who began making printed journals and radio programs for children in the northern portion of the state. These locally based, relevant, and culturally appropriate materials are well accepted by teachers and children alike. After deciding to expand its work to the rest of Queretaro, this group looked to teachers to help promote environmental education activities in their own communities.

The group decided that the best way to reach teachers was through a training course. With university faculty members and government technicians collaborating from the beginning, a course was designed that achieves the Ministry of Education standards.

Some teachers are attracted to the course because they sincerely want to learn more and teach their students about the environment. Others attend because completion can mean an increase in salary and free materials.

The project is beginning to affect one very important problem in the region: the mistrust of government agencies and messages. Because of a history of deception and corruption, few people trust employees of the Ministries of Ecology or Agriculture. Through this course, these Ministries improved their public image. Teachers and the communities learn that these technicians are involved in productive projects and have important information to share about environmental standards and protection. The joint activity is improving communication and perspectives among rural citizens and government technicians as they work together to achieve sustainable communities.

The Results

The project has received support from a variety of sources. For example, paper for the materials is donated by a local recycling factory, the Ministry of Education publishes the materials and sends them to rural school libraries, and university faculty members volunteer their time to teach. Over 200 teachers have taken the course, and more are waiting. Six course manuals have been published and three others are in development. There is also evidence that the environment is changing in these communities: More latrines have been built and more stoves used as a result of the course.

Preserving Traditions and Acting for the Future: Environmental Education and Sakha Youth

Valentina Dmitrieva
Public Information Center
Republic of Sakha, Russia

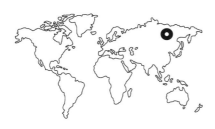

What Works

The most successful environmental education programs are developed locally by individual authors and educators.

The use of indigenous national traditions can help revive a culture's interest in and respect for nature.

Involving environmental youth groups in government and private sector activities provides the opportunity for youth to engage in practical solutions to resolve regional environmental problems.

City youth who are out of touch with nature can be reunited with the natural world through summer environmental camps and expeditions.

The realization of a state-sponsored, school-based environmental education program in Sakha has been limited by financial constraints. However, several extra-curricular programs have been successful in promoting environmental awareness and action in the region.

The Situation

The Republic of Sakha has a long tradition of comprehensive and compulsory environmental education programs. There is an understanding in Sakha that children should be encouraged to take direct action to protect the environment. Youth participate in various projects that monitor environmental conditions and standards.

The Project

Erkeyi, a republic-wide extra-curricular program aims to develop cultural and nature awareness among Sakha youth. The project (assisted with support from ISAR, the Institute for Soviet-American Relations) incorporates indigenous national traditions, customs, and holidays into environmental education programs. The aim of the activities is to expose youth to the relationship between the regional folk traditions and nature. Vocabulary words related to spiritual objects of nature and traditional customs are taught in an effort to promote both environmental awareness and the national language. City youth are exposed to the environment through participation in summer environmental camps and expeditions. During the expeditions, the youth pay respects to the spirits of water, forest, meadow, mountain, and fire, and promise to act according to the laws of nature and ask for support in their efforts. The national holiday, *Ysiakh*, is celebrated just before the hay harvest and incorporates environmental education activities.

Direct activity by youth to protect the environment is an integral part of environmental education in Sakha. Environmental youth groups have worked with government and private sector organizations on projects such as determining whether schools conform to sanitary and hygiene regulations, testing radiation, measuring vehicle emissions, investigating waste use methods, checking food standards, promoting environmentally sound products, and cleaning up pollution. Based on these experiences, the youth typically write a report and take part in environmental olympiads or youth conferences. Sometimes, local newspapers report on youth activities; in a few cases, the findings have served as the agent of change in improving regional environmental conditions.

(Translation by Miranda Lutyens)

"Action" for Growing Minds in Southern Africa

Stephen R. Murray
Action
Harare, Zimbabwe

What Works

Joint projects with approval from Ministries of Education encourage international cooperation and exchange.

Joint responsibility among the nations, with shared writing and pilot-testing responsibilities, solidifies the cooperation.

Sensitive issues are approached with a balanced and rational attitude.

Gender-based differences are probed and left open for discussion.

Teacher materials are provided in supplementary magazines, and workshops enable teachers to gain skills to use these materials.

Action is an environmental and health education project based in Harare, Zimbabwe. Through the format of a magazine, it researches, develops, and publishes education and training materials for children, teachers, and their communities.

The Situation

Rural educators in southern Africa often teach without textbooks, laboratories, equipment, or other resources. When textbooks are available, they are often written by experts in other countries, or even other continents, and therefore lack an important sensitivity to how rural people rely upon and use their local natural resources. A high priority for *Action* has been to develop locally relevant education materials with interesting, engaging activities that use available resources.

The Project

Begun in 1987, *Action* magazine is now read by about one million school children and 100,000 teachers in six nations of southern Africa: Botswana, Lesotho, Namibia, Swaziland, Zambia, and Zimbabwe. The information in *Action* magazine is written and pilot-tested with school children and teachers across the region before it is published, making certain that the information is appropriate and interesting. The cooperation of the six Ministries of Education and curriculum development offices makes it easier to develop, test, and distribute the material. The topics relate to the dependence of the communities of southern Africa on the natural resources around them. *Action's* approach to environmental education recognizes the inseparability of conservation, rural development, political empowerment, and survival; its training program enhances the work of community-based natural resource management programs.

The Results

Surveys and interviews with teachers, students, and distributors indicate that *Action* magazine is a widely read and well-regarded source of information about the environment and health. It is often used instead of a textbook and represents a replicable model for cost-effective curriculum development and international cooperation. One key ingredient of this success is the participation and dialog with students and teachers during the development of the materials. The magazine itself uses several guidelines: local knowledge is respected; the interests and behaviors of role models are open for discussion; and specific situations are used to introduce the larger context.

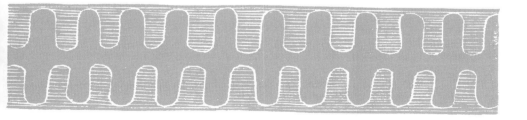

The Air Quality of Curitiba: Evaluating and Educating

Ziole Zanotto Malhadas
Federal University of Paran
Curitiba, Brazil

What Works

Elementary teachers and students are trained and motivated to conduct accurate air quality measurements using simple air quality devices.

An integrated process of research, evaluation, and education, including teachers, community members, and university faculty was used to develop the program.

Air quality is a relevant theme that can promote interdisciplinary, interactive environmental education activities in urban areas.

Universities can work successfully with communities and schools.

This interdisciplinary project involves over 12,000 teachers, young students, and university students in monitoring levels of air pollution. A series of educational activities increases community awareness and supports teacher training.

The Situation

Curitiba is a large, industrial city in Brazil. Although internationally famous for its modern public transportation system, Curitiba does have air pollution problems. Consequently, air quality is a relevant context for promoting broad, interdisciplinary environmental education. This pioneering project uses air as a theme, and helps to connect the community with the university by encouraging broad participation in research.

The Project

The ProAR project is a research project that simultaneously promotes environmental education, increases public awareness, motivates people to participate in solutions to air quality problems, and involves the university in a process of interactive learning in the community. In 1995, sampling devices were installed in 40 residences. In 1996, 30 primary schools received the device and training from university coordinators and undergraduate students. Teachers were trained by two university coordinators with the collaboration of three undergraduate students to measure levels of tropospheric ozone and particulates. The primary teachers developed additional interdisciplinary activities with their colleagues and involved all of the school children in the teaching and researching process. Newspaper and television news stories carry information gleaned from the sampling devices and help inform community members about air quality.

The Results

The program is extremely successful at generating interest, sharing knowledge about air quality, and involving members of several different educational institutions in a collaborative process of teaching and researching. After getting started with the ProAr program, most of the teachers involved in the program produced and implemented additional interdisciplinary class activities. For example, one teacher had students count passing cars to collect data for a mathematics, geography, and statistics lesson; and another used neighborhood trees to explore the connection between vegetation and air quality. Elementary students who participated in the month-long sampling process also produced letters, texts, drawings, and plays with their new knowledge. As a result of these successes, the Municipal Secretary of Education is trying to expand the program from 30 schools to all 122 municipal schools.

Along with the successes, the coordinators face a constant struggle with three simultaneous challenges: to obtain financial support for the program materials; to avoid conflicts with politicians who do not want information about air pollution to be revealed to the population; and to tolerate the traditional attitudes of some university members who are threatened by the idea that good research can be conducted by community members. Because of these challenges, a nongovernmental organization may be a better coordinator for the long-term project.

The results of the monitoring indicate that the ozone level in Curitiba varies from 20 to 320 ppb (parts per billion) and that particulate pollutants are significant only near the industrial zone. Air quality in Curitiba can no longer be ignored.

Changing Attitudes through EDUCAR, A Radio Environmental Education Program

Suyapa Dominguez Merlo and Jaime Bustillo
EDUECO
San Pedro Sula, Honduras

An innovative radio-based environmental education program, which included teacher training and accompanying educational materials, was launched in 27 banana plantation schools. The combination of a teacher guide, student workbooks, and radio broadcasts was previously unheard of in rural Honduras.

The Situation

After an initial series of three teacher workshops in environmental education for schools of the Tela Railroad Company (a banana plantation in Honduras), the company expressed interest in continuing environmental education efforts by radio. EDUCAR (Environmental Education Through the Radio) was designed to foster environmental awareness among students, to train teachers in environmental education methodologies, and to develop environmental education materials for

What Works

Radio is an effective way to teach students over a broad distance without losing educational quality.

Teachers seem more secure with environmental topics when they have print materials and a periodic radio program to use with their students.

Workshops for teachers are an important first step to implementing a successful new program.

Students seem to learn better when they are presented with a variety of learning modes, including listening, reading, observing, and doing activities related to the theme they study.

Teachers and students are an excellent link with the community and a good way to start changing attitudes in the area.

teachers and schools.

The Project

The project began with visits to the banana plantation schools to understand the teachers' and students' expectations about environmental education, and with reviewing the materials already in use. Based on this information, twenty 25-minute radio programs were designed. Accompanying materials were also created: student workbooks for each of three different grade clusters (1-2, 3-4, 5-6), a 265-page teacher guide, and ten radio spots to promote environmental messages. After the materials were prepared, three 3-day workshops for teachers from the 27 banana plantation schools were conducted to discuss educational methods and to address ways to use the written and audio environmental education materials. The project also provided radios to the schools. The programs aired twice a week in the months of June, July, and August. The cost of the project (US$30,000) equaled about $8 per participant.

The Results

Program designers observed the radio broadcasts in six schools, and the participating teachers and students completed surveys to rate the usefulness of the radio broadcasts and student workbooks. Observers noted positive changes of attitudes and behaviors, and participants rated the combination of methods and materials as highly successful and effective. Behavioral changes observed include students throwing less trash on the floor, parents not burning plastic while they cook tortillas, and teachers and students using a new environmental vocabulary.

The project points out that educators should not be prejudiced about funders and institutions. Although the banana company may know that the banana production process can be harmful to its workers, it was willing to fund a comprehensive environmental education program.

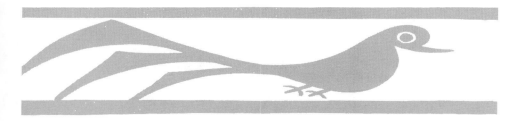

Implementing Education Programs to Conserve Biodiversity: Lessons from Mongolia

Jessica Bernstein
Education Consultant UNDP/GEF
Colorado, United States

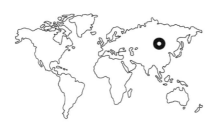

To help protect and promote biodiversity conservation in Mongolia, the Mongolian Biodiversity Project created, pilot tested, and distributed a biodiversity guidebook for primary and secondary school teachers.

The Situation

Mongolia occupies a critical ecological transition zone in Central Asia where the Gobi Desert, the Siberian taiga forest, the Altai mountains, and the Central Asian steppe converge. Many of these areas provide habitat for rare plants and animals of central and northern Asia. These include several endangered species such as the snow leopard, the Gobi bear, the argali or wild mountain sheep, the Mongolian subspecies of saiga, the white-naped crane, and the wild ass.

Mongolia is a vast and sparsely populated country of 2.5 million people. Half of the country's people are nomadic herders who travel by horse and camel to herd their sheep, cattle, and goats through an annual cycle of grasslands. However, as Mongolia

What Works

Conducting an accurate and thorough needs assessment is essential.

On-going roundtable discussions and seminars are effective ways to evaluate the program in early stages, providing guidance in design, production, and implementation.

Teacher training programs include several components: factual information about the environment, ideas for how to integrate environmental education into the required curriculum, and techniques for teaching interactively.

Involving ecology and conservation biology professionals in design makes the program accurate and informative.

Participation is necessary to facilitate local ownership of a project, yet teachers need incentives to participate.

The educational activities in the teacher guidebooks require few additional resources for conducting with students.

experiences a tremendous socioeconomic transformation, threats to its natural areas and fauna are rapidly increasing. Uncontrolled human activities—poaching, mining, deforestation, pollution, and livestock grazing—all threaten Mongolian biodiversity.

The Project

The Mongolia Biodiversity Project (MBP) is a collaborative effort to conserve Mongolia's biodiversity through improved laws, research, management, public awareness, education, and other conservation measures. The education element of this project involved increasing the level of biodiversity awareness among children ages 5-12 and their educators, developing country-specific materials for biodiversity education, training teachers to integrate biodiversity topics into the required curriculum, and building the capacity of educational and environmental institutions to develop and transfer effective biodiversity education.

Existing environmental education was limited to minimal units on agriculture and ecological regions of Mongolia. A coalition of individuals from government agencies, nongovernmental organizations, teachers, biologists, artists, and students worked to create a biodiversity activity guidebook, *Nature and Children*. This guidebook helped teachers easily integrate and adapt biodiversity activities into several subjects. The activities focus on student-centered, first-hand experiences. Lesson plans, student work pages, illustrations of endangered species, background information, glossary, and reference materials are included.

Pilot-testing helped determine that materials were appropriate for both rural and urban educators. Oral and written feedback on the activities, student reactions, and suggestions helped improve the materials. Master teachers from rural areas receive training and then conduct workshops with teachers in their region.

The Results

The MBP has begun to raise awareness and concern for Mongolia's biodiversity. Teachers who pilot-tested the materials responded very positively. They preferred the new, interactive teaching methods to their familiar, traditional techniques. They also noticed a marked increase in student participation during the *Nature and Children* lessons.

The popular guidebook has been distributed to teachers; the book has received accolades from Mongolians and international educators. The Ministry of Science and Education officially approved it in 1995 and the Ulaanbaatar Department of Education expressed interest in using it in a new curriculum structure. Other programs have adapted portions of the guidebook for their use.

6 ORGANIZING NONFORMAL ENVIRONMENTAL EDUCATION

Creative uses of media and a variety
of audiences, location, and sponsors
are hallmarks of nonformal environmental
education activities. Whether in national
parks or community centers, adults and
youth are learning about their environment.

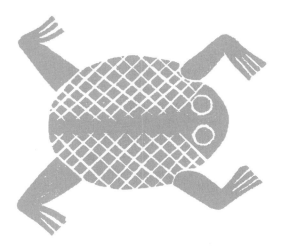

OUTREACH:
Disseminating and Evaluating Information Packets Worldwide

James V. Connor
OUTREACH
New Jersey, United States

What Works

Country organizers, key contacts, and multipliers perform an effective role of translating international materials to a local context and making these messages available over local media.

Local nongovernmental organizations are used to help disseminate information because they can adapt, translate, and distribute materials through existing media, and community and educational systems.

Assisting in the development of localized materials helps to create more relevant, interesting, and practical materials.

The OUTREACH Network produces packets of environmental and health information intended for young people in Africa, Asia, Latin America, the Caribbean, and the Pacific; they are distributed by local communicators, called multipliers.

The Situation

In low-income nations around the world, little information about environmental deterioration and personal health reaches the young or the disadvantaged. To address this need, a coalition of four environmental and educational organizations—World Wide Fund for Nature, United Nations Environment Programme, New York Zoological Society, and New York University—formed the OUTREACH Network. The goal of OUTREACH is to provide young people around the world with relevant and practical information on health and environmental issues, with the hope that these people would be able to make better decisions and take responsible actions at the local level. OUTREACH relies on local communicators, or multipliers, to translate, adapt, and disseminate this information through the most effective local media channels.

The Project

OUTREACH has produced and distributed over 100 information packets of copyright-free educational resources on environment and health issues such as wetlands, endangered species, water purification, energy, and seeds. Each packet contains about 40 pages printed in black-and-white for easy reproduction. Packets are sent free-of-charge to about 800 multipliers in the developing world. Multipliers are key communication contacts who adapt, translate, and disseminate OUTREACH messages to a broader group of people. They may be teacher trainers, journalists, radio broadcasters, nongovernmental organizations, or curriculum developers. In Ghana, for example, OUTREACH materials go to the teacher training colleges where science tutors give the materials to student teachers, who adapt the lessons for their classrooms. OUTREACH has also provided technical support to local organizations producing instructional materials in Kenya, Nigeria, Thailand, Jamaica, Indonesia, Bolivia, and southern Africa (see Action case on page 78).

Recently, OUTREACH has evaluated its strengths and world needs, and has decided to focus its efforts on reaching youth and women in low- and middle-income countries; it will develop a network of key communicators who work directly with youth and women in formal and nonformal systems and who can use OUTREACH's print materials. To achieve this aim, OUTREACH will conduct a needs assessment to understand better the environmental and health information needs of youth and women, begin an evaluation procedure to measure the effectiveness of the information supplied by OUTREACH, and develop a strong network of key communicators by working with country representatives in target nations.

Changes in Water Conservation Beliefs and Practices through After-School Programs in Jordan

Nancy Diamond and Orlando Hernández
GreenCOM Project
Washington DC, United States

An after-school-club curriculum for secondary schools in Jordan was designed to improve water conservation among students.

The Situation

Water scarcity is an increasingly serious problem in this desert country. All known sources of water have been tapped. Management of existing water resources and promotion of water-rationing programs are vital to ensuring adequate water resources. Many Jordanians perceive the water shortage problem to be beyond their control, or think such problems can only be solved by governmental negotiations with Syria and Israel, who share the use of the Jordan River.

The Project

To instill a sense of personal control over water usage and to spur Jordanian students and parents to action, the Royal Society for the Conservation of

What Works

Involvement of a local nongovernmental organization in curriculum development, implementation, and evaluation fosters local capacity development and sustains program implementation.

Involving teachers in the design of the curriculum increases the appropriateness of its content and its eventual use.

Appropriately developed, user-friendly manuals introduce teachers to effective environmental education techniques.

After-school clubs introduce environmental education content to interested students and teachers, and reach students' families to change behavior.

Nature (RSCN) developed a water conservation curriculum with technical assistance from the GreenCOM Project funded by the United States Agency for International Development. The curriculum was used by extracurricular environmental clubs in male and female single-sex secondary schools from January to April 1995.

The after-school program was an easier avenue to reach teachers and students than working through the Ministry of Education. Eco-Clubs allowed for information about environmental issues to be conveyed in an engaging atmosphere and shared with families. One unit of the curriculum engaged students in water conserving behaviors at home.

In a two-week workshop, a curriculum was adapted with assistance from master teachers, administrators, technicians, and nongovernmental organization representatives. Several teachers pilot-tested the curriculum activities. When the materials were completed and reproduced, RSCN conducted a workshop for club leaders to become familiar with activities and issues. The technique of teaching with interactive, engaging activities was new to these teachers.

The developers used gender-sensitive research to design and evaluate the program. This research provided important insights for identifying the content, evaluating the curriculum's impact, and redirecting activities.

The Results

The curriculum was evaluated with a survey of club leaders (teachers) and students who used the materials, and those from different schools who did not. Sixty percent of the teachers who received the curriculum and training implemented a majority of activities from all five units. Club leaders who participated devoted more activities to water-related topics and used more interactive teaching approaches than non-participating teachers. More female teachers used the unit on household water use than did male teachers.

The evaluation revealed that the curriculum had positive impacts on the knowledge, attitudes, beliefs, and practices of club members. Participating students had more positive scores on a set of questions than non-participating students, with boys showing higher scores than girls. Participating students made more suggestions about household water conservation to their parents than non-participating students; this behavior was reported by more boys than girls. In addition, participating students reported practicing more household water conservation behaviors than non-participating students.

It was evident that family behaviors changed with the school-based, club-sponsored activities. For example, more family discussions about water conservation (a precursor to action) occurred as a result of the activities.

Puppet Shows as a Tool in Environmental Education Programs

Flavio Linares
United States Peace Corps/Guatemala
Guatemala City, Guatemala

What Works

Environmental education that actively involves participants is successful in generating discussion around sensitive environmental issues.

Puppetry has a strong impact because it helps to present potentially controversial and sensitive issues through a neutral medium, and it is also entertaining.

Involving primary school teachers as narrators ensures that the audiences understand the messages.

Loud, clear voices by the characters increase audience understanding and help reinforce important messages.

A careful understanding of a culturally and linguistically diverse audience is important in developing appropriate messages.

The Environmental Management Project, operated by Peace Corps/Guatemala, assigns Peace Corps volunteers to work in environmental education, biological research, and ecotourism development. Puppetry is one method the project participants use to communicate environmental messages to ethnically, culturally, and linguistically diverse audiences.

The Situation

Guatemala, a country with rich biological and ecosystem diversity, faces serious problems from environmental degradation. Rapid forest destruction, coastal contamination, and depletion of wildlife populations are among the most serious problems. Throughout the country, the public is unaware of the country's environmental problems. There is a strong belief among environmental organizations that environmental education is necessary to increase the practice of sustainable environmental behaviors.

The Project

Over an 18-month period, volunteers and technicians of the Ecoquetzal Project of the Biosphere and Sustainable Development Association (BIDAS) carried out environmental education workshops for primary school teachers and led activities for women and small farmers in select communities. In planning these workshops and activities, project implementors selected puppetry as a learning tool based on their understanding of the communities' needs.

Creative skits were developed that addressed deforestation and its associated problems as the main themes. Identification of themes, messages, and objectives helped guide the development of the shows. The shows involved the audiences by asking for their active participation. Questions after the skits generated further discussion of the issues presented. The use of puppetry helped lighten the topic and engaged eager audiences. The local promoter answered questions and announced dates for future training courses and demonstrations after the skits.

The Results

The puppet shows reached 3,000 people from 20 schools and communities. Primary school teachers who participated were highly satisfied with the shows and they believed that the students and adults learned important information about the environment. The shows had a significant positive impact on the audience. Several months after the shows students still recited lines from the skits. Women and farmers who attended the performances have felt freer to ask about environmental issues, and others have been motivated to take action. Fifty farmers were trained in sustainable agriculture practices by BIDAS promoters and technicians.

Folk Media: A Nonformal Environmental Education Strategy in the Philippines

Roscela Pamela S. Poyatos
Protected Areas and Wildlife Bureau
Quezon City, Philippines

Through the Dalaw-Turo Nature Conservation and Awareness Outreach Program, staff members of the Protected Areas and Wildlife Bureau (PAWB) are trained to use interactive, engaging educational media to teach students and citizens about biodiversity and sustainable development.

The Situation

Dalaw-turo is a Filipino term that means "to visit and to teach." Begun in 1992, the Dalaw-Turo Program is an information, education, and communication component of a non-traditional outreach effort to teach students about biodiversity and sustainable development. Program staff initially visited schools near protected areas, and performed a stage play for students. The program currently uses different artistic methods to teach the public about the importance of protected areas and the need for responsible attitudes and strong commitment to environmental protection.

What Works

The program staff is trained to be responsive to the needs, value system, culture, and learning attitude of the local people.

Street theater, ecological tours, environmental games, exhibits, and lectures are effectively combined to create a positive learning environment.

The trained staff is motivated by being respected for individual talents, capabilities, and limitations; by consistently enhancing skills; and by listening to the audience.

Evaluation and needs assessments are built into the project at several stages, enabling project members to identify strengths and improve weak areas as the program evolves.

Dialects or multiple languages could be a communication barrier, but this challenge is overcome using visually based media, such as graphics and drama.

The Project

The Dalaw-Turo Program trains PAWB staff in successful educational techniques. A ten-day training module has been developed that includes: values orientation, communication skills, acting skills, materials production, performance evaluation, communication campaign design, and regional implementation. The training program not only teaches technical information and the creative teaching methods staff can use, but also increases staff motivation and commitment to pursuing environmental education activities. By the end of the workshop, participants are able to produce lecture materials, environmental games and skits, eco-tours, and interpretive materials for their protected area. Other Dalaw-Turo offerings include ecological tours in National Parks and protected areas, materials development, community visits with elders, and school visits. Enhancement training is provided to upgrade skills and keep staff current in the program.

The Results

Monitoring and evaluation have been integral parts of the Dalaw-Turo Program. Informal interviews are conducted with people who live near protected areas to assess their level of awareness about the significance of their park. Pre-program and post-program surveys are conducted before and after Dalaw-Turo school visits with students. Teachers are also asked to complete evaluations forms to comment on the program. Five months after a school visit, PAWB staff members monitor the action plans that the school and community have undertaken. Other environmental activities are also monitored. These evaluations indicate that 96% of the respondents have adapted the teaching methods of Dalaw-Turo and that 83% have been motivated to embark on nature conservation projects. Positive results are apparent in all the communities that have been visited by the Dalaw-Turo approach; local people are more receptive and responsive to the environmental issues being presented to them.

To date, the program has trained 244 field staff from the Department of Environment and Natural Resources covering all regions of the Philippines. A pilot test of a training module for teachers was conducted in 1996, and the program may evolve into a teacher-training phase in the near future.

Using Environmental Education Activities to Reach Aboriginal School Children in Taroko National Park, Taiwan

Homer C. Wu
Chaoyang University of Technology
Taichung, Taiwan

An environmental education program at Taroko National Park was designed to involve nearby schoolchildren, including aboriginal students, helping them to understand the conservation goals of the newly established park.

The Situation

Taiwan is a nation that considers education of paramount importance. Although environmental education is becoming more established, little has been specifically directed at aboriginal students. Taroko National Park, near the city of Hualien, was established in 1986 to protect Taroko gorge with its marble cliffs, waterfalls, mountain peaks, and virgin forests, and the majestic landscape surrounding it. The park is located in an aboriginal community called Atayal. The Atayal people strongly opposed the creation of the park because they believed their hunting and slash-and-burn farming lifestyle would

What Works

Interpretative programs at a park effectively engage youth in activities that teach them about ecological principles and conservation goals.

Because a program designed by members of one culture does not necessarily resonate with members of another culture, evaluations are used to identify aspects of the program that need improvement.

The program helps enhance students' school experience by providing resources that are beyond the means of the normal classroom.

be changed by it.

The Project

An environmental education program was developed in the new Taroko National Park to teach conservation to fourth-, fifth-, and sixth-grade students, including Atayal students. In 1994, the Park initiated the program by making classroom visits to surrounding schools. With funding from the Ministry of Education in 1995, the park sent invitation letters to surrounding elementary schools encouraging them to visit the park. The response was overwhelming.

Programs were created to emphasize the Earth's dynamic cycles of light, air, and water; food webs; nature observation; and hands-on experiences. Each program included the concept of conservation in hopes of minimizing illegal activities such as hunting and mining within the park.

The Results

At the end of the activities, students were asked to complete a questionnaire. About 82% of the respondents indicated they were satisfied with the program; 97% of them stated that as a result of the program, they will cherish natural resources in their daily life. The evaluations also indicated areas where the programs can be improved.

The evaluations were extremely helpful in confirming that environmental education programs can help build sensitivity, awareness, and understanding about the natural world. The responses also revealed that the programs were not particularly effective for the Atayal students. Changes in the programs will be made to reflect the Atayal world view, culture, and traditions.

Connecting Wetland Ecosystems, Cultures, and Migratory Birds through Sister Schools

Heather Johnson and Cathy Rezabeck
United States Fish and Wildlife Service
Alaska, United States

The Shorebird Sister Schools Program combines birds, science, environmental issues, and computer technology in an exciting school-based program. By making up-to-date information on migrating arctic shorebirds available to those with e-mail or Internet access, a variety of sightings and activities are occurring across the flyway each migration season.

The Situation

The Shorebird Sister Schools Program teaches students about the fascinating migration of Arctic nesting shorebirds and the importance of conserving wetland habitats for their survival. The program is a teaching unit within the Arctic Nesting Shorebirds Education Program. The full program consists of several printed resources: a curriculum, a flyway map, a shorebird guide, and an Internet migration tracking program.

What Works

Starting out small and expanding over time allowed the project to work out problems, prevent their reoccurrence as the project expanded, and predict more accurate project costs and timelines.

A multidisciplinary design team, including biologists, teachers, environmental education specialists, and managers, ensures that a variety of perspectives are represented.

Flexibility in project design and structure ensures that unforeseen situations and problems can be incorporated or corrected.

Setting goals and objectives helps keep the project on target when they are used for monitoring progress and growth.

Using technology (like the Internet) attracts some people to the program, but varied educational media (like booklets, posters, and field trips) means more people can be served.

The Project

The Shorebird Sister Schools Program uses the Internet to teach students about wetland habitats, shorebird migration and cultures throughout the Western Hemisphere. As the birds fly from southern latitudes to their nesting grounds in the Arctic, observers enter information on the Internet data pages.

The program began in 1994 in Homer, Alaska, with 14 schools linked through America Online. In 1996, the program expanded and developed a World Wide Web site with open participation. A list server was created to allow two-way correspondence between teachers, students, biologists, and shorebird enthusiasts from across the Western Hemisphere, with different types of Internet access.

The Results

The Internet has rapidly increased participation in the Shorebird Sister Schools Program. The program has expanded from 14 schools in the United States in 1995 to more than 300 individuals who subscribe to the list server. The Shorebird Sister Schools site received more than 1,000 hits per week on its World Wide Web site during the peak of the spring migration. Twenty-one countries are now represented in the program. The project constantly receives positive comments about the quality of the information available on the home page.

7 BUILDING LOCAL CAPACITY

In international development projects, without a doubt, the most worthy goal is to leave expertise behind. Environmental education and communication programs often provide local residents with the skills to improve their lives and perhaps continue similar education and communication programs. The development of new leaders is a key ingredient to success.

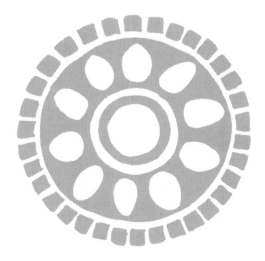

Female Adult Literacy in Rural Pakistan

Sabiha S. Daudi
Ohio State University
Ohio, United States

What Works

Initial interviews and discussions with literacy educators help to gain their commitment and to determine the need for content related to local environmental concerns.

Environmental literacy materials are most successful when developed with input from teachers and others active in basic literacy programs.

The World Conservation Union (IUCN) in Pakistan developed an environmental education primer to increase literacy skills among rural women of Punjab and to create awareness about relevant environmental issues.

Qualitative methods of assessment through informal interviews and group discussions give valuable information for revising the materials and can lead to further activities.

The Situation

The rural people of Punjab, Pakistan, are farmers who also collect wood and fodder from forests and fish the local waters. Their village lifestyle is negatively influenced by pollution from nearby industry, forest degradation, increasing population, and the absence of environmental management plans. In rural Punjab, women not only nurture their families, but also manage water, food, forest, livestock, fuel, and sanitation. The Adult Basic Education Services (ABES) program has actively developed literacy programs in the area for over 45 years, with literacy activities for women tending to focus on health and agriculture topics. IUCN in

Involvement of local nongovernmental organizations supports the smooth implementation of the literacy activities.

Pakistan proposed to develop an environmental component for the well-established ABES literacy program.

The Project

The objectives of the project were to create an awareness about local environmental concerns through environmental education of the women in rural villages; to provide adult educators with an opportunity to teach about the local environment; and to provide ways to explain local environmental issues so villagers can understand their role and their responsibility for finding solutions. Women of all ages were invited to participate in the project; as the project evolved, males were also invited to join. Participants set the time and venue: usually at a neighbor's home for several hours after sunset. The project provided reading materials at a nominal cost. Qualitative methods, not exams, were used to monitor the project.

The Results

The environmental component was successfully integrated into the established literacy program. The materials were carefully developed, with appropriate formative discussions and pilot-testing. Teachers were motivated to include environmental issues in their other lesson plans, and the popular environmental primer has been distributed to other nongovernmental organizations active in literacy programs. Based on the positive results of the primer, three booklets for neo-literate readers are planned for different literacy levels.

The project might have had greater success if it had sought a stronger commitment from the literacy program, and had involved other social workers and nongovernmental organizations who could have supported the project. Implementation might also have been greater if the project had included local educators, leaders, elders, and school teachers in creating a community consensus for this important activity.

Dissemination of Environmental Materials and Training

Volodymyr Tykhyi
Environmental Education and Information Center
Kiev, Ukraine

The Environmental Education and Information Center (EEIC) has taken on several activities to help coordinate various aspects of environmental education in the Ukraine.

The Situation

Ukraine is new to environmental education and only recently began using ecological approaches in some schools and universities. Ukrainian education, however, does have a strong tradition of field activities in biology, nature conservation, and ecological tourism that could be considered a firm foundation for environmental education. Many teachers would like to teach about the environment, but they realize their activities must be coordinated to provide the best learning opportunities for students.

There is a strong need for national coordination that allows for the exchange of information and opinions,

What Works

Organizational support and general training (planning, team building, communication skills) should be provided and funded to develop nongovernmental institutions.

Attention and funding should go to in-country coordination of work and dissemination of results.

Existing capacities should be identified and strengthened, allowing the use of existing links and expertise, leaving expertise in-country when the project is completed, and bypassing the long lead-time required to establish new organizations.

There should be extensive cooperation and communication among donors within the region.

the establishment of dialogue between various levels of educators, and the stimulation of creative energies. Although an environmental nongovernmental organization might play this role, these organizations are relatively new in Ukraine (appearing at the time of democratization), and tend to compete for limited resources rather than work together. Neither the Ministry of Education nor the teaching community, which has no professional association for teachers of ecology or geography, has taken on the challenge.

The Project

The Environmental Education and Information Center (EEIC) was formed in 1993 by the Ministry of Environmental Protection and the University of Kyiv Mohyla Academy and has since become a nonprofit public organization. EEIC has taken on several activities to help coordinate various aspects of environmental education in the Ukraine. These activities include inviting representatives of different sectors to attend US Environmental Protection Agency training seminars; distributing technical packages of environmental education materials to schools, universities, and libraries (see the next case on EE-TIPs); serving as a clearinghouse for translated materials and experiences; maintaining an e-mail conference on the creation of new Regional Environmental Centers in CIS countries; and publishing environmental booklets for students.

The Results

EEICs efforts have had mixed success. The training seminars were extremely successful. The email conference stimulated a great deal of productive dialogue, and electronic communication promises many exciting opportunities. The booklets, however, did not stimulate the expected cooperation and activity, perhaps because neither funds nor time were available for follow-up activities.

EE-TIPs: Making the Most of U.S. Environmental Education Resource Distribution in Eastern and Central Europe

Joan Haley
North American Association for Environmental Education
Washington DC, United States

What Works

Asking recipients what they want is an excellent way to select among available resources.

Partnering with agencies and organizations already working in the region helps expand the network, extend resources, and reduce inefficiencies.

Empowering country coordinators to oversee the selection, distribution, and use of materials is essential when the coordinating organization is not located in that region.

A training workshop to familiarize educators with materials helps ensure the collection will be used.

In-country workshops with materials enhance the dissemination and exchange of materials and ideas.

Through funding from the United States Environmental Protection Agency (EPA), the North American Association for Environmental Education (NAAEE) developed 200 mini-libraries for Eastern and Central Europe, each containing over 50 top-quality publications.

The Situation

A few countries have developed a great many environmental education materials, while other countries have a huge need for materials. The Environmental Education Technical Information Packages (EE-TIPs) project worked to meet this need by providing materials to countries in Eastern and Central Europe. Participating countries included Poland, Czech Republic, Slovakia, Bulgaria, Hungary, Romania, Lithuania, Latvia, and Estonia. The project faced three major challenges: how to select materials and ensure they were appropriate for the region; how to ensure that the materials got into the right hands; and, perhaps most challenging, how to encourage full use of the materials.

The Project

After asking environmental education professionals in the United States to identify recommended publications, a sample EE-TIPs box was prepared. Environmental education professionals in Eastern and Central Europe then reviewed this collection and selected items most relevant for educators in their region. Reviewers, for the most part, selected items with:

- clear and colorful graphics
- easy-to-read text, not too technical or dense
- how-to information and not theoretical or process-oriented information
- a focus on priority environmental issues, such as water pollution
- innovative and fun teaching methods.

Their suggestions narrowed the list of materials from over 100 resources to approximately 50. The resulting materials included in EE-TIPs provide educators with current information on environmental issues, innovative teaching techniques, effective environmental education tools and skills, networking opportunities, legislative models, and fundraising techniques.

To distribute 200 sets of materials to people who could effectively use them, NAAEE partnered with the United States Peace Corps, which works with existing environmental education networks in Eastern and Central Europe. Volunteer coordinators from each of the participating countries served as in-country liaisons to select sites based on how well a proposed site could provide educators with access to the materials, provide training, and promote the materials and environmental education. Peace Corps and NAAEE conducted a training-of-trainers workshop to increase familiarity with the EE-TIPs resources. Participants also exchanged details on the successes and challenges of environmental education in their respective countries.

An introductory brochure for the box was developed in each language, describing how to use the EE-TIPs materials. Each box also included a detailed bibliography with contact information.

The Results

Two hundred sets of EE-TIPs boxes and brochures have been distributed to selected sites in Eastern and Central Europe. NAAEE is working with recipients to find out which materials are used most frequently; who tends to use the materials; and what kind of training, promotion techniques, and organizational support seem to encourage their use. A Spanish-language EE-TIPs collection is being planned for educators in the United States and Latin America.

The Challenge of Changing Teaching Styles in Rural Zimbabwe

Kathy Greaves Stiles
Harare, Zimbabwe

A two-year project to document the acceptance of a problem-solving teaching style in primary Zimbabwe classrooms resulted in an exploration into why the change did not happen. The insights reveal reasons that transfer of pedagogical practice may not occur in teacher education programs.

The Situation

From 1991 to 1994 a project in Zimbabwe attempted to implement a problem-solving approach in environmental science in rural primary schools. Teacher change was a particularly important variable. The initial year of testing showed that students' problem-solving skills remained unchanged. Teachers did not use the problem-solving pedagogy often or effectively. Teachers were confused about what they were to do, or misinterpreted the methodology and taught something different with great confidence. The evaluation effort then explored why teachers did not change teaching styles.

What Works

The context in which the pedagogy was created and the one in which it is to be transferred must be considered, including how the systems differ, how the incentive structures differ, how the students' and parents' needs differ, and whether the program is relevant.

Consideration should be given to the type of pre-service and in-service education that is offered to teachers in the new context. Ideally, it should be very similar to the type of pedagogy that is introduced.

In-service training should involve and empower learners rather than be a traditional and paternalistic, though expedient, format.

Participatory research techniques, such as biographies and discussions, can help participants and researchers develop themselves.

The Results

The teachers realized there were strong inhibitors to changing their teaching style, stemming from both external and internal sources. The external inhibitors included a centralized government education system that uses a national syllabus, national tests, English language, and a limiting period of time; and community and school factors that stem from economic influences such as poverty, class size, and the separation of school and community. The internal inhibitors included a lack of subject matter knowledge, lack of experience as a student under this pedagogy, and lack of English language ability.

During the process of participatory research to explore these inhibitors, the teachers became quite critically reflective and assertive. They became skilled in expressing their ideas and in understanding the barriers to change. In the future, a careful review of the system may help to design an in-service program or to adapt a methodology that would be more successful. For example, it might be important to examine teachers' motivation for change when they are required to administer student exams involving factual, rote answers, and when student pass rates help to determine their own salary and upward mobility.

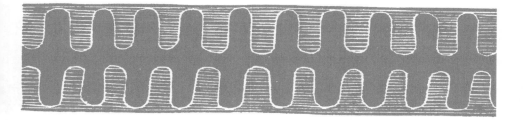

Second Generation Leadership: A Nicaragua-Wisconsin Partners Environmental Leadership Project

Joe Passineau and Dan Sivek
University of Wisconsin-Stevens Point
Wisconsin, United States

What Works

Cross-cultural exchange and travel programs can dramatically alter a person's world view and foster a global environmental perspective; such experiences should be encouraged.

Participant selection and the training process are critical to the program's success.

Follow-up support is needed to ensure completion of community environmental action projects.

Funding support is needed from multiple partnerships for travel and out-of-country experiences.

The Nicaragua-Wisconsin Environmental Leadership Project is a cultural exchange project of the Nicaragua/Wisconsin Partners of America with the goal of fostering environmental knowledge and community action skills.

The Situation

Similar environmental problems plague both Nicaragua and Wisconsin, including water pollution, waste disposal issues, and habitat loss. Residents in both regions are concerned about these problems and are motivated to improve their environments. Youth groups, citizen groups, and teachers are working in both countries to engage people in quality environmental education programs. An environmental education exchange program for teachers, students, and community leaders was designed to work with these organizations to foster awareness of ecological interdependence and to build action-taking skills.

The Project

In 1995, 20 high school teachers, community leaders, and students participated in a six-week education program with three weeks in Nicaragua and three weeks in Wisconsin. This pilot exchange was designed to increase environmental literacy and skills in team work, volunteerism, and citizen participation; to enhance leadership skills and confidence to improve environmental conditions; and to strengthen cultural awareness and second-language skills. After an orientation session including cultural and natural resource information, each country's organizers arranged an environmental education seminar with field experiences and expert presentations, a homestay experience for visiting participants, and a community environmental action project that would develop during the seminar.

The Results

Evaluations of the program indicate that it was highly successful. Although fewer participants attended than desired, having a small group increased the sense of camaraderie and the speed at which friendships were built. Evaluation tools included application essays describing personal goals and final essays on personal growth and insights; observations of participant enthusiasm, involvement, culture shock, and readjustment behaviors; participant surveys on the program content; and participant journals.

With such a small group, results are difficult to quantify. Qualitative indications of its success include the facts that two students have changed majors into environmental fields and one student has applied for funds to conduct a litter management project; that participants in the pilot program are willing to assist in program development, homestays, and follow-up support for future programs; and that the program is being developed, and has been funded, for a three-year project.

Based on the results of the pilot exchange, the project is being expanded to include more training in leadership skill development, more narrowly focused environmental action projects, and increased emphasis on project evaluation and participant follow-up. In addition, the project may be split into separate leadership programs for mid-career community leaders and teachers with students.

Environmental Management in the Kyrgyz Republic

John H. Baldwin
University of Oregon
Oregon, United States

To improve the environmental management capabilities of the Kyrgyz Republic's Ministry of Environment, this project provided training in environmental impact assessment, environmental management, and the use of communications technology.

The Situation

The Kyrgyz Republic (or Kyrgyzistan) is a newly-independent state in central Asia, west of China and south of Kazakhstan. Only 7% of the land is arable, with cotton and tobacco grown on irrigated land in the south, and grains produced in the foothills. Nearly half of the land area is pasture for sheep and goats. Abundant hydroelectric potential and significant mineral deposits are among the nation's promising resources. Managing these resources, however, is challenging. The dissolution of the Soviet Union left the Kyrgyz Republic with enormous responsibilities and little in the way of

What Works

The development of an efficient, integrated, decentralized environmental management system includes cooperation, information-sharing, training, monitoring, analysis, and effective enforcement.

Training programs are most effective when they include research on critical environmental issues, data sources, monitoring systems, facilities, and education programs.

Involving a newly organized nongovernmental organization helps to build capacity and trust within the republic.

resources, experience, or management systems. Land degradation, inefficient mining practices, poor water management, exploitation of forest resources, and threats to biodiversity are among the most pressing environmental issues.

The Project

The Asian Development Bank funded a project conducted by the AGRA Earth and Environmental Limited Institute of Alberta, Canada, to assist the Kyrgyz Republic in developing legislation, regulations, environmental monitoring, an environmental management system, and training. In 1996, a two-week workshop was offered to managers that focused on environmental impact assessments, environmental management, and the use of computer technology (especially the Internet).

The Results

Additional support to the Kyrgyz Republic is still needed, but the preliminary foundation for improved environmental management has been established. The project is providing information and training materials to: develop a national conservation and development program; improve the efficiency of environmental monitoring and management; promote the democratization of information; provide support for newly formed nongovernmental organizations; and foster cooperation and communication between the government and citizen groups.

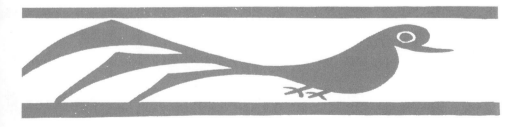

Summary

Throughout this volume, several themes emerge:

- It is critically important to involve leaders and participants in the design of environmental education and communication programs and materials;

- High quality programs are developed with careful and thorough data collection and evaluation processes;

- Cooperative efforts across sectors help insure high quality and long-term stability of programs;

- A careful balance between the efficiency of using existing materials and developing pride and ownership of new, original materials must be struck;

- Good work takes time; and

- There are many different ways to do it.

The programs represented here are indicative of creative, successful projects across the globe. More can be done, and more funding can make existing programs more powerful. A great deal is known about what works, and there is much to be discovered. As environmental issues grow increasingly critical, environmental education and communication programs become vital tools for sharing information, implementing policy, or achieving change. These cases and guidelines are provided to spark ideas, encourage development, and share success.

Region and Country Index

Africa

Benin	26
Senegal	40
Tanzania	30
Zimbabwe	78, 108

South America

Bolivia	52
Brazil	20, 24, 38, 56, 80
Ecuador	28
Guyana	52
Peru	56

Central America

Costa Rica	58
Guatemala	68, 92
Honduras	82
Nicaragua	110

North America

Canada	52
Mexico	66, 74
United States	98, 106, 110

Europe

Bulgaria	44, 106
Czech Republic	106
Estonia	106
Greece	22
Hungary	72, 106
Italy	22
Latvia	106
Lithuania	106
Poland	106
Portugal	22
Romania	106
Russia	42, 46, 76
Scotland	22
Slovakia	106
Spain	22
Ukraine	104, 106
United Kingdom	22

Middle East

Egypt	50
Jordan	90

Asia

India	36
Indonesia	32, 54
Kyrgyz Republic	112
Mongolia	84
Pakistan	62, 102
Philippines	64, 94
Russia Far East	42, 76
Taiwan	96

Multinational Projects

22, 52, 78, 88, 98, 106

Contact List

Page	Contact	Organization and Address
20	Margaret Cymerys	8 Main Street, Box 194 Point San Quentin, CA 94964 USA Work Phone: 415-256-9427 Fax: 415-460-1681
22	Marco Paliano	Worldwide Fund for Nature - Italy Via Garigliano 57 Rome 00198, ITALY Work Phone: 068-449-7360
24	Marcus Polette	Universidade do Vale do Itajal Oceanografia R. Uruguai 458-Fazenda, CX Postal 360, Itajai, Santa Catarina, BRAZIL Work Phone: 55-473-447-541 Fax: 55-473-447-633
26	Constant Dangbegnon	Universite Nationale du Benin 04 BP 1386, Cotonou, BENIN Work Phone: 229-300-276 Fax: 229-300-276
28	Clarice Strang	Fundacion Pro-Pueblo Casilla 09-01-4243, Guayaquil, ECUADOR Work Phone: 593-4-901-208 Fax: 593-4-901-195
30	Mary Shuma	WWF Tanzania Programme Office P.O. Box 63117, Dar Es Salaam, TANZANIA Work Phone: 255-51-75346/72455 Fax: 255-51-75535
32	W.J. 'Rocky' Rohwedder	Department of Enviromental Studies and Planning Sonoma State University Rohnert Park, CA 94928 USA Work Phone: 1-707-664-2249 Fax: 1-707-664-3920
36	Abdul Ghafoor Ghaznawi	Asian Institute for Environmental Education House No. 2, Street 64, Islamabad, F-8/4, PAKISTAN Work Phone: 92-51-260-561
38	Lou Ann Dietz	WWF/Latin American and Caribbean Programs 1250 24th Street, NW, Washington, DC 20037-1175, USA Work Phone: 1-202-778-9611 Fax: 1-202-296-5348

40	Mamadou Diaw	US Peace Corps/Senegal BP 2534, Dakar, SENEGAL Work Phone: 221-23-71-78 Fax: 221-22-93-81
42	Margarita Arutiunian	Institute of Teachers — Retraining and Qualification Improvement 5 Angarskaya Street, Khabarovsk, 680006, RUSSIA Work Phone: 7-4212-36-20-12
44	Veleslava Tzakova	TIME-Ecoprojects 58 Yanko Sakazov Street, Sofia, 1504, BULGARIA Work Phone: 359-287-3252
46	Andrea Deri	Institute for Sustainable Communities 56 College Streey, Montpelier, VT 05602, USA Work Phone: 1-802-229-2912 Fax: 1-802-229-2919
50, 90	Orlando Hernández	Academy for Educational Development/GreenCOM 1255 23rd Street, NW, Washington, DC 20037, USA Work Phone: 1-202-884-8872 Fax: 1-202-884-8997
52, 56	Haroldo Castro	Conservation International 501 M Street, NW, Suite 200, Washington, DC 20037, USA Work Phone: 1-202-973-2210 Fax: 1-202-331-9328
54	Katarina Panji	WWF Indonesia Programme Jl. Kramat Pela No.3, Gandaria Utara, Jakarta, 12140, INDONESIA Work Phone: 62-21-7203095/7245766/7256501 Fax: 62-21-7395907
56	see 52	
58	Guillermo Canessa Mora Luis Fernando Rojas Osvaldo Valerín	The Costa Rica Civic Foundation Apartado 1546-1002, San Jose, COSTA RICA Work Phone: 506-226-2570 Fax: 506-226-2570
62	Syed Jamil Kazmi	Society for Conservation and Protection of Environment B-150, Block 13, D/2 Gulshan-e-Iqbal, Karachi, 75300 PAKISTAN Work Phone: 92-21-496-5042/497-6459 Fax: 92-21-496-4001

64	Chris Seubert	Global Vision Inc. 11802 Saddlerock Road, Silver Spring, MD 20902, USA Work Phone: 1-301-593-5649 Fax: 1-301-593-8469
66	Elena Chavarria	Pronatura Sonora Apartado Postal 484 Guaymas, Sonora 85400 MEXICO Work Phone: 52-622-11505 Fax: 52-622-11505
68	Myriam Monterroso	ARCAS Santa Elena, Peten, GUATEMALA Work Phone: 502-9-500-077 Fax: 502-9-500-077
72	Bill Helin	U.S. Peace Corps 1919 K Street, N.W. Washington, D.C. 20526 USA 202-606-9480 202-606-3024
74	Lizbeth Baqueiro	Consejo de Mejoramiento Ambiental Sierra Gorda 25, Pathe, Queretaro CP76020, MEXICO Work Phone: 52-4223-1500/4882 Fax: 52-4223-1160
76	Valentina Dmitrieva	Public Ecological Center of the Republic of Sakha 12/71 Kulakovskogo St., Yakutsk, 677007, RUSSIA Work Phone: 7-411-2-44-61-38 Fax: 7-411-2-44-61-38
78	Stephen R. Murray	Action Box 4696, Harare, ZIMBABWE Work Phone: 263-4-705-859/724-401 Fax: 263-4-795-150
80	Ziole Zanotto Malhadas	Universidade Federal do Paran NIMAD, Av. Munhoz de Rocha, 98, Curitiba, Paran 80035-000, BRAZIL Work Phone: 55-41-252-4461 Fax: 55-41-366-2723
82	Suyapa Dominguez Merlo	EDUECO P.O. Box 353, San Pedro Sula, HONDURAS Work Phone and Fax: 504-51-3956
84	Jessica Bernstein	7000 Sunshine Canyon Boulder, CO 80302 USA Work Phone: 303-444-5237 Fax: 303-444-2499

88	James V. Connor	Outreach P.O. Box 2875, Branchville, NJ 07826, USA Work Phone and Fax: 1-201-948-5185
90	See 50	
92	Flavio Linares	Peace Corps/Guatemala 8a Calle 6-55, Zona 9, Guatemala City, GUATEMALA Work Phone: 502-334-8263 Fax: 502-334-4121
94	Roscela P. S. Poyatos	Dalaw-Turo Nature Conservation and Awareness Outreach Program Protected Areas and Wildlife Bureau, Quezon Ave. Diliman, Quezon City, PHILIPPINES Work Phone: 632-924-60-31/2/3/4/5 Fax: 632-924-01-09
96	Homer C. Wu	Department of Leisure, Recreation and Tourism Management Chaoyang University of Technology, 168, Gifeng East Road, Wufeng Taichung County, 413, TAIWAN Work Phone: 886-4-3323000 x7453 Fax: 886-4-3742363
98	Heather L. Johnson	U.S. Fish and Wildlife Service 1011 East Tudor Road, Anchorage, Alaska 99503, USA Work Phone: 1-907-786-3367 Fax: 1-907-786-3635
102	Sabiha S. Daudi	School of Natural Resources, Ohio State University 700 Ackerman Rd., Suite 235, Columbus, OH 43202, USA Work Phone: 1-614-292-8436 Fax: 1-614-481-8483
104	Volodymyr Tykhyi	Environmental Education and Communication Center P.O. Box 136, Kyiv, 254070, UKRAINE Work Phone: 380-44-290-6563 Fax: 380-44-274-2417
106	Joan Haley	NAAEE 1255 23rd Street, NW, Suite 400, Washington, DC 20037, USA Work Phone: 1-202-884-8913 Fax: 1-202-884-8701

108   Kathy Greaves Stiles   Consultant in EE and Ed. Research
P.O. Box 949, Harare, ZIMBABWE
Work Phone: 263-4-301720
Fax: 263-4-791202

110   Dan Sivek   College of Natural Resources
University of Wisconsin - Stevens Point
Stevens Point, WI 54481, USA
Work Phone: 1-715-346-2028
Fax: 1-715-346-3025

112   John H. Baldwin   Institute for a Sustainable Development
130 Hendricks Hall, 5247 University of Oregon,
Eugene, Oregon 97403-5247, USA
Work Phone: 1-541-346-3895
Fax: 1-541-346-2040

Brian A. Day,   GreenCOM
GreenCom Director   Academy for Educational Development
1875 Connecticut Ave, NW
Washington, DC 20009 USA
Work Phone: 1-202-884-8700
Fax: 1-202-884-8701

Martha Monroe,   School of Forest Resources and Conservation
Editor   University of Florida
PO Box 110410
Gainnesville, FL 32611-0410 USA
Work Phone: 1-352-846-0878
Fax: 1-352-846-1277

Carole Douglis,   GreenCOM
Editorial Consultant   Academy for Educational Development
1875 Connecticut Ave, NW
Washington, DC 20009 USA
Work Phone: 1-202-884-8700
Fax: 1-202-884-8701